Early American Wars

Battle on the Plains
The United States Plains Wars

Robert O'Neill, Series Editor; and Charles M. Robinson III

ROSEN
PUBLISHING
New York

This edition published in 2011 by:

The Rosen Publishing Group, Inc.
29 East 21st Street
New York, NY 10010

Library of Congress Cataloging-in-Publication Data

Robinson, Charles M., 1949–
Battle on the plains: the United States plains wars / Charles M. Robinson, III.
    p. cm.—(Early American wars)
Originally published under title: The Plains Wars, 1757–1900. Oxford : Osprey Pub., 2003.
Includes bibliographical references and index.
ISBN 978-1-4488-1334-6 (library binding)
1. Indians of North America—Great Plains—Wars. 2. Indians of North America—Wars—1750–1815. 3. Indians of North America—Wars—1815–1875. 4. Red River War, 1874–1875. 5. Dakota Indians—Wars, 1876. I. Robinson, Charles M., 1949– Plains Wars, 1757–1900. II. Title.
E78.G73R63 2011
978.004'97—dc22

    2010032930

Manufactured in the United States of America

CPSIA Compliance Information: Batch #W11YA: For further information, contact Rosen Publishing, New York, New York, at 1-800-237-9932.

Copyright © 2003 Osprey Publishing Limited. First published in paperback by Osprey Publishing Limited.

On the cover: Custer's Last Stand. (Whitney Gallery of Western Art)

Contents

Introduction

The Plains Wars between the United States and the various Native American tribes and nations were not wars in the conventional sense. They were a series of ongoing clashes, culminating in two large-scale military actions: the Red River War of 1874–75 in the Southern Plains, and the Great Sioux War of 1876–77 in the Northern Plains. Although they are generally lumped together under the heading of "Native American Wars," the conflicts in the Northern and Southern Plains began in different eras, and often involved different peoples and motives. In some ways, these wars by region were oddly similar to World War II, in which one conflict raged in Europe and North Africa, while an entirely separate war was being fought in the Pacific and Far East. The wars between the federal

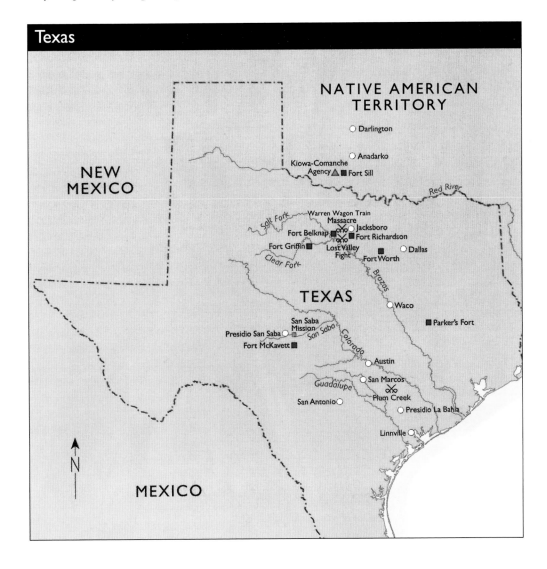

Texas

The Hunkpapa chief Sitting Bull led the resistance against the Fort Laramie Treaty and, together with Crazy Horse, has become a modern symbol of Native American determination. There are no authenticated photos of Crazy Horse, although it is known that he was pale and freckled, with red hair, unusual traits that Native Americans believe endow a person with a special spirituality. (Author's collection)

government and the Southern Plains tribes were essentially inherited, having their origins a century earlier when much of the region belonged to Spain. The Northern Plains wars were uniquely American, rising from the expansion of the whites into the territory west of the Mississippi River.

Plains Native Americans were warriors. Long before the coming of the white man, they warred with each other, just as people do throughout the world. The Cheyenne and the Pawnee had no more love for each other than the Frenchman may have had for the German in Europe, and acted accordingly. Death in close combat with an enemy, with one's deeds of valor told and retold by the campfires, was preferable to growing too old to hunt or fight, and sitting in the lodge, cold, toothless, and feeble. Cheyenne warriors dressed especially well for battle or in other times of danger, so that if they died, they would look their best upon entering the next world (Grinnell, *1956*, 12; Marquis, 83). The fighting tradition has been carried into modern times, with service in Vietnam, Desert Storm, and Afghanistan giving young men a chance to prove themselves as warriors. Some of the old warrior societies, such as the Kiowa Black Leggings, have been resurrected as veterans' organizations.

Some Native Americans allied themselves with the whites, as an opportunity to settle ancient grievances against other Native Americans. In a council with Brigadier General George Crook in June 1876, a Crow chief gave a lengthy indictment of the Lakotas and Cheyennes. The Crows, Arikaras, Shoshones, and others offered themselves as scouts for the army as a chance of gaining revenge for past abuses (Bourke, Diary, 5:388–91). Such was often the case when the government enlisted Native American

auxiliaries. The scouts themselves had few illusions about white ambitions; they had simply weighed up the odds, and considered the government as the lesser of two evils.

Whites, likewise, pitted Native Americans against other whites. In the Southern Plains, French influence was evident in Native American conflicts with Spain, because both countries had territorial ambitions in the region. In the North, commercial rivalries over the fur trade prompted American and Canadian interests to vie against each other for influence over the local tribes. The Native Americans themselves, recognizing these animosities, played one white faction against another for their own advantage.

Until 1849, management of Native American affairs was the responsibility of the War Department. That year, however, jurisdiction was transferred to the newly created Department of the Interior. The result was that while the Native Americans theoretically were under civilian administration, the military continued to be responsible for suppressing outbreaks. Because these outbreaks were so frequent and political corruption visibly rampant, the soldiers were convinced that the Interior Department was incapable of handling the situation. Thus Native American affairs became mired in interdepartmental rivalries, divided responsibilities, and lack of coordination or cooperation, and would remain so until the end of the Native American Wars. Many soldiers disliked Native American fighting. General Crook viewed both Native Americans and soldiers as victims, forced to fight each other to vindicate failed policies (Priest, Chapter 2; Robinson, *2001*, 220).

Besides the rivalries, Native American affairs were complicated by inconsistent government policies. On the one hand, the government tried to buy peace by issuing goods to the more warlike tribes. Native Americans quickly learned that if they stayed on their reservations and minded their own business, they would be neglected, but if they committed depredations, they would be rewarded (United States Department of the Interior). Too many depredations, however, brought a military response, but very often a campaign was hindered on the brink of success, by yet another government policy of negotiation.

When General U.S. Grant was inaugurated as president in 1869, he hoped to solve the problem of corruption by replacing civilian agency appointees with officers demobilized under the Army Reduction Act. General W.T. Sherman, who replaced Grant as general-in-chief of the army, believed it would have been "a change for the better, but most distasteful to members of Congress who looked to these appointments as part of their proper patronage." To prevent the appointments, congress approved a bill canceling the commission of any army officer who served in a civilian position.

Refusing to be defeated, Grant then turned the management of Native American affairs over to the various religious denominations. Agents appointed by the churches, he believed, would be above reproach, and would inspire the Native Americans by enlightened example. The Board of Native American Commissioners was created as a quasi-official agency to oversee distribution of the Native American appropriation. Native Americans on the reservations would be under the exclusive control of the agents, unless an agent specifically requested military intervention. Officially, this was known as the Peace Policy. Rather than solve the problem, however, the new approach only prolonged the agony, because, in common with less developed warrior societies throughout the world, Native Americans took inconsistency, indecision, and forbearance

A contemporary drawing shows the nation's four most famous Native American fighters: (clockwise from top) Brigadier General George Crook, Lieutenant Colonel George Armstrong Custer; Colonel Ranald S. Mackenzie, and Colonel Nelson A. Miles. (Author's collection)

as signs of weakness, and behaved accordingly. (Tatum, 133; Sherman, 926–27; Leckie, 134–35)

Ultimately altruism failed. Two major wars finished the Native Americans as independent people, but today, the issues raised by those wars remain unresolved.

Chronology

Early Chronology

1731–48 Clashes between Spaniards and Plains Apaches

1758 **March 16** Massacre of San Sabá Mission, Texas

1767 Rubi's inspection realigns Texas defenses; isolated presidios abandoned

1781–90 Ugalde's punitive expeditions against Plains Apaches

1821 Americans begin settling Texas

1820s–70s Fighting between Texas settlers and Plains tribes

1823 Arikara War on the Missouri River

1836 **May 19** Raid on Parker's Fort, Texas

1840 Comanche War in Texas

1840s–50s Settlers moving through Platte Valley disrupt Native American life

1846 Formal entry of Republic of Texas into the Union makes federal government responsible for defense

1849 Management of Native Americans transferred from War Department to Interior Department

1849–79 Gold and silver rushes in California, Nevada, Colorado, Montana, and South Dakota bring miners and prospectors into the plains

1851 First Fort Laramie Treaty attempts to pacify Northern Plains Native Americans; government begins acquisition of Santee Sioux lands in Minnesota

1853 Fort Atkinson Treaty tries to obtain peace with Southern Plains Native Americans

1854 **August 19** Grattan Massacre, near Fort Laramie, Wyoming, initiates Sioux Wars

1855–56 Harney expedition on the Northern Plains

1861–65 Civil War. Majority of federal troops withdrawn from frontier

1862 **August 18–September 26** Santee uprising in Minnesota

1863–68 Increased raids on western frontier

1864 **Summer** Sibley and Sully expeditions on the Northern Plains

October 13 Elm Creek Raid, Young County, Texas

November 25 First fight at Adobe Walls, Texas

November 29 Sand Creek Massacre of Cheyennes by Colorado troops

1865 Sully and Connor expeditions on the Northern Plains

1869 President Grant implements Peace Policy

Southern Plains chronology

1865 Little Arkansas Treaty

1867 **Spring and Summer** Hancock's War

1868 Medicine Lodge Treaty

1868–69 Cheyenne War, Kansas and Oklahoma

1868 **September 17** Beecher's Island fight

November 27 Custer attacks Native American villages on the Washita

1870–78 Slaughter of the buffalo

1871 **May 18** Warren Wagon Train Massacre, Texas; Kiowa Chiefs Satanta and Big Tree subsequently imprisoned

1874–75 Red River War on Southern Plains

Northern Plains chronology

1866–68 Red Cloud War, Wyoming and Montana

1868 Fort Laramie Treaty

1876–77 Great Sioux War

Subsequent events

1878–79 Cheyenne Outbreak
1879 Suit by Ponca chief Standing Bear
determines that Native Americans
have legal standing in court
Indian Rights movement gains impetus
White River Ute uprising
1887 Dawes Act divides reservations into
individual land holdings
1889 Break-up of Great Sioux Reservation
1889–90 Rise of the Ghost Dance Religion
1890 **December 29** Wounded Knee
Massacre of Lakotas by federal troops

1924 American Indian Nationality Act gives
Native Americans full citizenship
1934 Indian Reorganization Act allows
limited self-government and cultural
freedom
1944 National Congress of American
Indians organizes
1960s–70s Rise of American Indian
Movement
1969 Native Americans occupy Alcatraz
1972 Native Americans seize Bureau
of Indian Affairs Building in
Washington
1973 Outbreak at Wounded Knee

North and South

The Southern Plains

The first serious clashes between Plains Native Americans and whites occurred during the 18th century on the Southern Plains. As defined by William H. Leckie in his classic work *The Military Conquest of the Southern Plains*, the region occupies an area from the Platte river in the north to the Rio Grande in the south, and from the Rocky Mountains in the west to about the 98th meridian in the east.

The first Europeans to enter the plains were the Spaniards. Although the Coronado Expedition explored the territory in the 1530s, it was almost two centuries before they made any serious attempt to settle. To them, the plains meant the west central part of modern Texas. The reasons for ignoring Texas for so long were economic—it did not appear to offer mineral wealth to exploit, or large congregations of Native American souls to save. The reasons for ultimately settling the province were strategic. It formed a barrier that protected the rich mining regions to the south and west. The primary threat was the French, who already occupied Canada and were rapidly colonizing the Mississippi valley. Thus the Plains Wars in Texas assumed the shape of a contest of empires, which became intertwined with existing rivalries between native tribes.

The first hint of trouble came when word reached the Spanish settlements that a French colony had been established on the Texas coast. This was the ill-fated expedition of René Robert Cavelier, Sieur de la Salle, and though it failed, its mere presence was enough to throw Spain into a panic. An initial attempt to establish a Spanish presence in the province in the 1690s failed, but the permanent French colonization of the Lower Mississippi at the beginning of the 18th century made further efforts imperative. By

1720, a string of missions stretched through eastern Texas, anchored at the edge of the plains by a mission, a presidio (frontier defense fort), and a town that ultimately became San Antonio (Fontana, 75–77, 122).

The Spanish occupation of Texas came in the wake of the introduction of the horse to the Great Plains tribes. This revolutionized Native American life, giving them unprecedented mobility, and allowing the various tribes to expand their range. The result was ruthless intertribal wars over hunting grounds, and territorial domain. The most powerful were the Comanches and Wichitas, who pushed the weaker Plains Apaches southward, into the areas of Spanish settlement. The Apaches, in turn, raided the settlements, stealing horses, plundering, and murdering. By 1731, they had become so aggressive that they were able to attack the horse corral of the Presidio of San Antonio, and beat back a relief detail sent from the fort. In response, Governor Juan Antonio Bustillo of Coahuila, whose jurisdiction included Texas, organized a punitive expedition composed of veteran Native American fighters. In 1732, Bustillo's troops attacked an Apache encampment, killing about 200, capturing 30 women and children, and recovering 700 stolen horses. The Apaches, however, fought with a ferocity that the soldiers had never before experienced. Additionally, they realized this was not the main band. Aware that the Native Americans could attack, and possibly even destroy, the presidio, town, and missions virtually at will, the soldiers petitioned the government to negotiate a peace. They were supported by the commandant of the presidio, Juan Antonio Perez de Almazon, and the president of the San Antonio Mission, Fray Gabriel de Vergara, the latter of whom feared a general uprising and massacre similar to what had happened

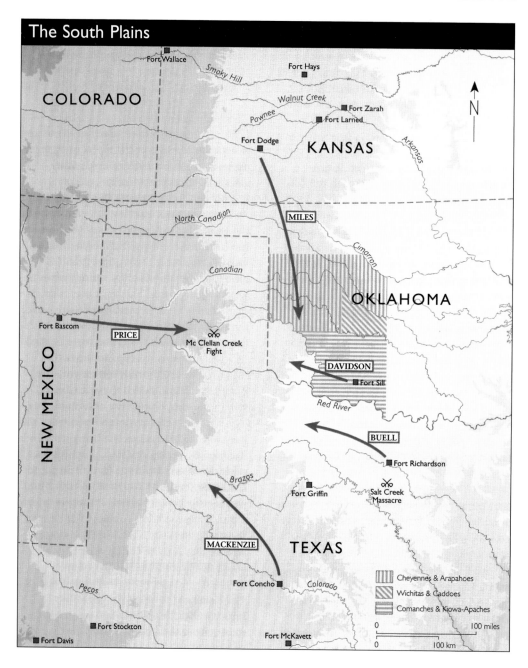

The South Plains

COLORADO

Fort Wallace

Smoky Hill

Fort Hays

Walnut Creek

Fort Zarah

Pawnee

Fort Larned

Fort Dodge

KANSAS

Arkansas

N

North Canadian

MILES

Canadian

Cimarron

OKLAHOMA

Fort Bascom

PRICE

Mc Clellan Creek Fight

NEW MEXICO

DAVIDSON

Fort Sill

Red River

BUELL

Fort Richardson

Brazos

Fort Griffin

Salt Creek Massacre

MACKENZIE

TEXAS

Pecos

Fort Concho

Colorado

Cheyennes & Arapahoes

Wichitas & Caddoes

Comanches & Kiowa-Apaches

0   100 miles

Fort Stockton

Fort McKavett

0   100 km

Fort Davis

in New Mexico in 1680. Despite these fears, little could be done, and Bustillo's punitive expedition was the first of three that would be undertaken against the Apaches between 1732 and 1748 (Simpson, xvi–xviii).

The Apache response was to play two enemies—Spaniards and Comanches—against each other. In late 1755, they began drifting in to a newly established mission and presidio near the present city of San Marcos, until more than a thousand had congregated. Their piety was lukewarm, just enough to make the priests hopeful. Their real motive appears to have been to seek Spanish protection from the Comanches, but they kept enough of a front so that the priests were encouraged. Because the local environment would not support such a large

Ruins of the San Sabá Presidio at Menard, Texas. The stone fortress was built after the massacre of 1758 to replace the existing stockade, and was partially reconstructed for the Texas Centennial in 1936. (Author's collection)

population, the priests petitioned the government to permanently relocate the mission and presidio to the San Sabá river, near the present city of Menard. San Sabá, it was hoped, would be the first of a chain of missions extending from San Antonio to Santa Fe, in New Mexico (Weddle, 35–37).

The San Sabá project was doomed from the start. The mood of the Apaches was questionable, at least to Colonel Diego Ortiz Parilla, a seasoned Native American fighter who was to command the presidio. When a delegation of Lipan Apaches arrived in San Antonio to discuss the project, the watchful Parilla suspected treachery. He was also uneasy about the coequal authority between himself and the president of the proposed mission, the strong-willed Fray Alonso Giraldo de Terreros, which he believed would create contradiction and confusion in a crisis. Already, the priests were quarreling among themselves. Nevertheless, the expedition got under way, arriving at the designated site on the San Sabá river on April 15, 1757. Despite the assurances of the Lipans in San Antonio, not a single Native American was there to meet them (Weddle, 44–50).

To the suspicious Colonel Parilla, the absence of the Native Americans indicated a fool's errand, and he urged the abandonment of the project. The priests, however, overruled him, and construction began on the mission, officially christened Santa Cruz de San Sabá, and the fort, designated the Presidio of San Luis de las Amarillas in honor of the reigning viceroy, the Marqués de las Amarillas. The priests were as suspicious of the soldiers as Parilla was of the Apaches. A few years earlier, a mission on the San Xavier (now San Gabriel) river had failed, in part because the soldiers, inspired by their commander, had appropriated the wives and daughters of the Native American neophytes. To guard against such abuses, the new mission was located 3 miles (5 km) downstream, and on the opposite side of the river from the presidio. While this might prevent military corruption, it also placed the mission too far away for aid when the time came.

About mid-June, some 3,000 Apaches appeared. They advised the priests, however, that they had not come to congregate, but were hunting buffalo. Their mood was sullen, and they spoke of war against the Comanches and the Hasinais (Weddle uses the term "Tejas" for Hasinai throughout, but "Tejas" is a colloquial term and specifically denotes a branch of the Hasinais living in the Neches-Angelina area of east Texas, far removed from the area under consideration [see Bolton, 53]) to avenge a recent attack against them. They advised the priests, however, that they planned to return and congregate, once the hunt was over and the Comanche–Hasinai raid had been avenged. No one is certain what the Apaches did during their absence, but they may have boasted of an alliance with the Spaniards, and during fighting may have lost some articles the Spaniards had given them. Whatever the case, their enemies believed the Spaniards had thrown in with the Apaches, and this sealed the doom of San Sabá. At the mission, meanwhile, the lack of Native American neophytes made it increasingly obvious the project was failing. Several of the priests returned to Mexico, and those remaining felt Terreros, the mission president, had deceived them. As autumn approached, various bands of Apaches came through, paused long enough to take advantage of the mission hospitality, and continued southward, giving the impression of fleeing. Rumors reached Terreros and Parilla that the northern tribes were banding together to destroy the Apaches, erroneously presuming that they had congregated at the mission (Weddle, Part 2).

As time passed, a respect grew between Parilla and Terreros, and they increasingly consulted each other on their respective goals which, in Parilla's case, was pacification, and in Terreros', the saving of souls. The priests ministered to the neophytes, while Parilla made it evident that the ministry could be backed by military force, if necessary. Although Terreros complained to the viceroy that the Native Americans' "promises of submission are sometimes pretexts for delay" he added that Parilla's "personally directed management … has protected them and decreased their antagonism." Nevertheless, he and Parilla believed that they personally should appear at court to explain to the viceroy the requirements necessary for a complete subjugation. Terreros' letter was dated February 13, 1758. By the time it reached the court in Mexico City, it was a moot point. Terreros was dead and the mission destroyed (Terreros to Amarillas, in Simpson, 1–3).

On February 25, Native Americans stampeded the horses in the presidio pasture. Sergeant Francisco Yruegas took 14 soldiers in pursuit, but after 12 days recovered only one live horse. Upon returning, he reported large numbers of Native Americans armed for battle. Parilla sent a detail to warn the escort of a supply train bound for San Antonio. The detail was attacked and four soldiers wounded, but they managed to reach the train. Smoke signals were seen in the north and east. On March 15 Parilla urged the priests to come to the presidio for protection. Terreros refused, apparently convinced the raid on the pasture and the attack on the troops were isolated incidents. Parilla left a guard of eight soldiers with two light cannon, ammunition, and muskets, then returned to the presidio.

At dawn the next day about 2,000 Comanches, Hasinais, Tonkawas, Bidais, and other allied tribes rushed the mission. They were painted for war, many carried modern firearms, sabers, and lances, and some were dressed in the style of the French military. Some 300 managed to get into the courtyard. Terreros and another priest, Fray José de Santiesteban, were killed, along with a soldier and two civilians. The others fought their way to the buildings, where they barricaded themselves in while the Native Americans plundered the mission. Then, the raiders set fire to the stockade, hoping it would consume the survivors in their refuges.

A relief column from the presidio encountered a band of heavily armed Native Americans on the road, and three soldiers were killed in the first volley of musket fire. Returning to the fort, they encountered mission Native Americans with a tale of slaughter. Convinced the mission was beyond aid, Parilla prepared the presidio for defense. That night, a sergeant took a detail to the mission, but found the Native Americans alert. Nevertheless, the soldiers rescued the survivors, who had managed to slip out of the buildings in small groups under cover of darkness. Two days later, the Native Americans withdrew (Weddle, Part 2).

The exact number of people killed at San Sabá is not known, but probably did not exceed 10 (Weddle, 88–89). This was small as massacres go, but the impact was great. The mission was doomed from the start, the victim of intertribal conflicts and the rivalries of empires. The organization and arms of the Native Americans left no doubt in anyone's mind that they were, in the words of the governor of Coahuila, "instigated by foreign political agents," specifically the French (Angel de Martos y Navarrete to Toribio de Guevara, in Simpson, 17).

The disaster marked the limit of Spain's imperial ambitions. It also inaugurated full-scale warfare between Native Americans and whites on the Southern Plains. Fighting would continue, passed on from Spain to other powers, for almost 120 years.

The Northern Plains

For the purposes of this book, the domain of the Northern Plains Native Americans extends from the Canadian border to the Platte river of Nebraska, and from the Rocky Mountains to approximately the Mississippi river. In fact, the Northern Plains extend well into Canada, and the Native Americans of the United States crossed over frequently. To them, Canada was "Grandmother's Land," so-called because of the portraits of an aging Queen Victoria that stared down at them from the walls of government outposts. Canada was a refuge in times of trouble with the United States, because US troops were hesitant to risk British wrath by crossing the border, nor was Great Britain likely to permit it. Thus, the boundary became a "Medicine Line,"

that offered a sort of magical protection once the Native Americans crossed it.

The most powerful of the Northern Plains tribes were the Western, or Lakota Sioux and their allies, the Cheyennes. The Lakotas, perhaps the largest Native American nation in the United States, were divided into seven tribes, Oglala, Brulé, Hunkpapa, Miniconjou, Blackfeet, Two Kettles, and Sans Arcs. Each had its own specific territory, although each summer they all met for an annual council that brought thousands of people together.

The Lewis and Clark Expedition established a permanent contact between the Native Americans and outsiders from the east. The age of the mountain man, which came in the wake of Lewis and Clark, introduced the Plains tribes to a plethora of newcomers. The effect was unnerving to the Native Americans, who resented the intrusion of trappers into their territories. Ambushes became common, and a trapping brigade's horse herd offered an incentive for theft. The mountain men themselves relied on old tribal grievances, often allying with one tribe against another (Hanson, 7).

One of the first tribes to react was the Arikara (or Ree) of the Upper Missouri River. In the spring of 1823, a group of Rees got into a dispute with a band of Missouri Fur Company traders, and two Native Americans were killed. In retaliation, on June 2, 1823, several hundred Rees attacked a trapping expedition led by William H. Ashley, about 600 miles (950 km) upriver from Council Bluffs, Iowa. Fifteen trappers were killed and 12 others wounded. Forced downriver, Ashley sent a message to Fort Atkinson, Nebraska, and a punitive expedition was mounted under Colonel Henry Leavenworth. The expedition, consisting of 200 infantrymen with artillery, about 700 Sioux allies, and 100 or more trappers, bombarded the Ree village, but Leavenworth allowed the inhabitants to escape. His failure to pursue and destroy the Native Americans was a serious loss of prestige for the whites among the Upper Missouri tribes, who thereafter were less hesitant to attack and, for a time,

The Presidio de Nuestra Senora de Loreto, better known as La Bahia, in Goliad, was one of the strongest Spanish frontier defense works, and the best preserved Spanish interior fort in the United States. The chapel is original, as are the lower portions of most of the walls. (Author's collection)

even managed to close the upper river to American trade (Utley, *Encyclopedia*, 16–17; Anonymous, 157–58).

While the trappers fought the Upper Missouri tribes, the Native Americans of the Platte valley and surrounding region resented the mass movement of whites across the plains toward Oregon and California. By the early 1840s, the sheer numbers of transients became threatening, particularly to the great Lakota Sioux tribes, who were accustomed to dominating by sheer number. Francis Parkman, Jr., who visited the Lakotas at the time, wrote (137):

Until within a year or two, when the emigrants began to pass through their country on the way to Oregon, they had seen no whites except the handful employed about the Fur Company's posts. They esteemed them a wise people, inferior only to themselves ... But when the swarm of Meneaska, *with their oxen and wagons, began to invade them, their astonishment was unbounded. They could scarcely believe that the earth contained such a multitude of white men. Their wonder is now giving way to indignation; and the result, unless vigilantly guarded against, may be lamentable in the extreme.*

This large movement of people actually threatened the Native American way of life. It drove game away from traditional hunting grounds, forcing the tribes to move farther afield in search of food. By 1845, much of the buffalo had been driven out of the Platte valley, requiring the Lakotas to hunt west of the Laramie Mountains and in the range of their traditional enemies, the Utes and the Shoshones. Another point of contention was settlement. On the eastern edge of the Great Plains, the encroachment of permanent white residents forced more Native Americans into smaller areas, throwing mutually antagonistic tribes into close contact with each other. War became inevitable (DeLand, 15:33–34; Myers, Folder 10).

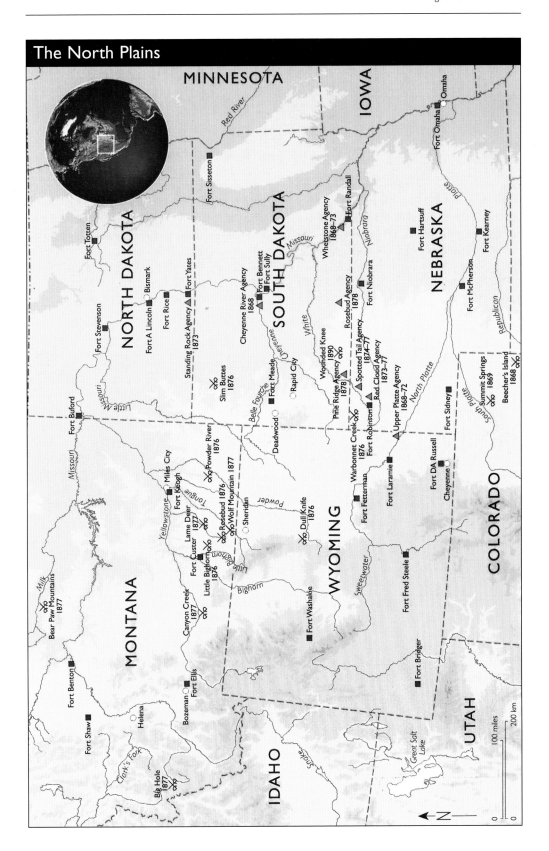

The North Plains

The soldier and the warrior

The Plains Native American mode of war

War was a means by which a warrior gained prestige, honor, and plunder. Individual combat was highly esteemed, and trophies of battle highly prized. Yet this individualism brought certain collective risk. Plains Native Americans were largely nomadic and tribal, and generally functioned in small bands. A dead warrior could not be replaced until a young boy reached fighting age, generally in his mid-teens. On the other hand, they realized that dead soldiers would be replaced immediately, often with a public outcry for vengeance. Consequently, in organized fighting, Native Americans preferred hit-and-run raids rather than open battle. Raiding itself was calculated on a cost–benefit basis. It was not worth losing several warriors just to obtain two or three scalps, but it was well worth the loss to obtain a herd of horses (Myers, Folder 10).

One best understands Native American thought when one looks at the exceptions, which is to say direct confrontations with the enemy. At Adobe Walls, Texas, in 1874, and the Rosebud, in Montana, in 1876, the Native Americans had a clear advantage. Yet each time, they broke off fighting when their losses began to mount. In the battle of the Little Bighorn, in which five companies of Seventh Cavalry were annihilated, the Native Americans were purely on the defensive.

There was no single standard for a Native American warrior. Each tribe or national group had its own customs and traditions. A Northern Cheyenne warrior generally retired from active combat about the age of 40, assuming of course, that he had a son who could take his place in the battle line. Although retired warriors would participate in battle as spectators, staying in the rear, singing war songs and shouting encouragement, actual fighting was left to younger men with more stamina and agility (Marquis, *n.d.*, 118–19). In other tribes, however, a warrior might fight well into old age. The Kiowa war chief Satank was in his 70s at the time of his last raid in 1871. Likewise, in 1876, the septuagenarian Washakie led his Shoshones as scouts for General Crook's Bighorn and Yellowstone Expedition, which culminated in the battle of the Rosebud.

Weapons

Traditional Native American weapons could be divided into five basic types—striking, cutting, piercing, defensive weapons, and symbolic weapons. Striking weapons included such things as clubs, tomahawks, axes, and whips, while knives were used as cutting weapons, and arrows and lances for piercing. In many cases, Native American warfare had a ritual as well as practical significance, so that Native Americans also had decorative ceremonial equipment, like headgear, war shirts, and even face and body paint, which would bring protection, enhance bravery, or otherwise give their wearers an edge. Somewhere in between the practical and the ceremonial were defensive weapons that included shields and armor (Taylor, 2001, 6–10). With the introduction of firearms and steel weapons, defensive gear became more symbolic than useful, although a hard, well-reinforced shield of smooth

The Tonkawa chief Chiahook, also known as "Charley" or "Charley Johnson," headed the Native American scouts attached to Fort Griffin, Texas. Many Native Americans served the government in an effort to settle ancient grievances against other tribes. Tonkawas were especially hated because they cannibalized the bodies of slain enemies. (Texas State Library and Archives)

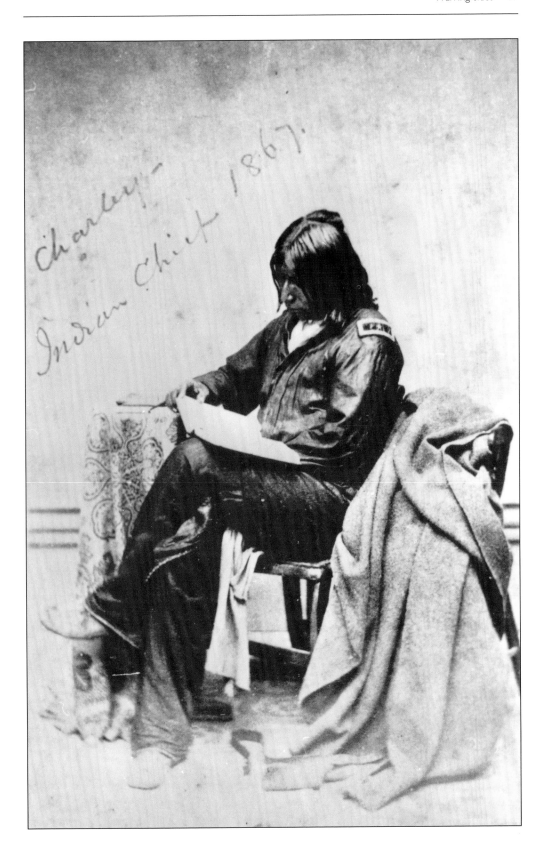

The ruthless Kiowa war chief Satank was arrested for his part in the Warren Wagon Train Massacre in Texas in 1871. Rather than return to Texas for trial, he jumped a guard at Fort Sill, Oklahoma, and was killed. (National Archives)

rawhide could still deflect a lance or even a ball from the early muskets (Simpson, xvi).

Like any warrior culture, Plains Native Americans often endowed their fighting equipment with special powers. Shields were thought to be particularly potent, and the men who made them were in touch with the spirit world. The Kiowa war chief Satanta, who died in 1878, carried a special "sun shield," one of six made in the 1790s by the powerful medicine man Black Horse, and the modern Kiowas still believe in its power (Grinnell, 1972, 1:192–93; Robinson, 1998, 24–26).

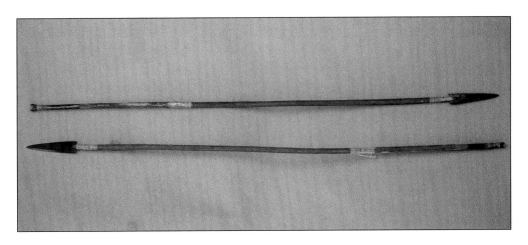

Plains Native American arrows with metal points probably obtained by trade. (Author's collection)

The government, through its Native American agents, issued guns for hunting, but unlicensed traders also made a lucrative business of selling the most modern firearms. Often, Native American warriors had better weapons than the soldiers had. Nevertheless, while a Native American was deadly with a bow, his aim with a firearm often was haphazard except at close range (Carleton, *Prairie Logbooks*, 271). Despite long familiarity with firearms, it was not until the latter part of the era that they became completely comfortable with them in combat, preferring instead the bow, lance, and shield for close-in fighting. A warrior gained battle honor by risking himself against the enemy. "Counting coup" – physically striking an enemy, living or dead—brought the greatest glory of all. Several warriors might "count coup" on the same enemy, but the supreme honor went to the one who struck first, and he vehemently defended his claim against any challenger (Grinnell, *Cheyenne Native Americans*, 2:30ff.).

The frontier soldier

The annexation of Texas in 1845 gave the United States Army an abrupt introduction into Plains Native American warfare with no time to prepare. Previously, as new areas were opened to settlement, the army went in, removed the local Native Americans, and concentrated them on reservations before serious clashes developed with incoming settlers. In Texas, however, the United States suddenly assumed responsibility for defending a heavily settled and populated state whose citizens viewed themselves as perpetually at war with the Plains tribes. The entire cavalry arm of the army consisted of two regiments of dragoons, and one of mounted rifles. The remainder of the troops was infantry and artillery. Consequently, infantry was sent to subdue mounted Native Americans, and with no previous experience, the US soldier had to improvise as he went along. Not until after the Civil War, which brought a reorganization and expansion of the cavalry arm, was the American soldier really able to meet a Native American on equal terms (Robinson, 2000, 105).

Officers had to contend with an enemy that did not fight by the generally accepted methods of war. West Point trained them to fight traditional battles against comparably trained field armies. This had served them well during the Mexican and Civil wars, and so they resisted change. One of Crook's aides, Lieutenant John Gregory Bourke, observed, "We have much to learn from the savage in the matter of Cavalry training; the trouble is our prejudices of education are so deeply rooted, common sense and observation have no permission to assert themselves" (Bourke, Diary, 6:597). Many officers were contemptuous of Native American hit-and-run tactics, later learning to their sorrow—that is not surviving to learn—how totally effective these tactics could be.

The Native American fighting soldier also faced public disdain. Americans, with their citizen-soldier heritage, have always been

Model 1904 McClellan military saddle. The McClellan was introduced in 1859 and, in various modifications, continues to serve US mounted troops. (Author's collection)

suspicious of professionals. The soldier of the civil war was generally a member of a volunteer unit drawn from his home county or state. He had the support, indeed the blessing, of his community. The regular soldier, on the other hand, had no home but the army. Many were drawn from the urban poor, or from immigrants, some of whom had served in foreign armies, and others who were unable to find employment upon arrival in the United States. The bloody nature of Native American warfare was repugnant to the civilized Eastern press,

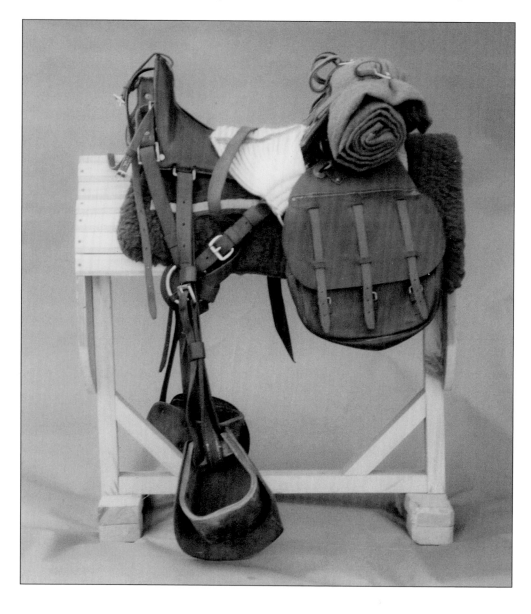

which often did not make the distinction between atrocities committed by vindictive local militias, and government policy executed by the regulars (Rickey, 24–25).

On post, bugles governed the soldier's life, with a specific call for each duty. A typical day might begin with reveille and stable call at daybreak. At 7:00 AM the soldier had breakfast. Drill, which after stable call was the most hated part of the day, ran from 7:30 AM at 8:30 AM. Guard was mounted at 9:30 AM, and those not on guard had fatigue duty for the remainder of the morning. There was another stable call at 4:00 PM, with retreat at sundown, fatigue at 8:15 PM, Taps at 8:45 PM, and guard inspection and mounting at 9:00 PM (Robinson, 1992, 43).

In his leisure time, a soldier might wander into one of the towns that frequently grew up in the vicinity of a military post. Sometimes these towns were well developed, with economic factors other than the army. Often, though, they were merely "hogtowns," shantytowns that existed solely to pander to the soldier's needs and vices. Either way, he could find gamblers, saloonkeepers, and "soiled doves," all willing to separate him from his hard-earned pay. The volatile combination of liquor, money, and women could lead to illness or violence. In March 1875, one post surgeon reported (United States Department of War, Office of the Surgeon General):

The habits of the Men might be materially improved by the removal of the number of Lewd Women living in the vicinity of the post. The Soldiers not only become demoralized by frequenting these resorts but some of them have already contracted venereal diseases and one soldier was wounded by a pistol ball in one of these drunken haunts.

Arms and equipment

The US soldier on the frontier was poorly clad for the task facing him. When the Civil War ended, the government still had massive

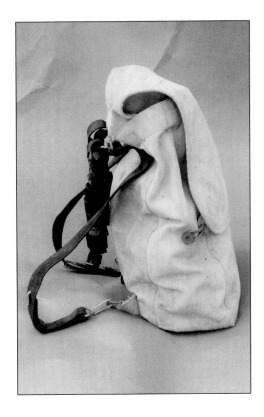

The model 1878 infantry pack was typical of military issue designed by Ordnance officers in the east who knew little about western field conditions. (Author's collection)

stores of uniforms and equipment. That, together with a reduction of the army by two-thirds within five years of the wars' end, convinced Congress there was no need to appropriate money for new clothing until the existing stockpiles were exhausted. Because of contractors profiteering during the war, however, much of it was ill-fitting or defective, and in 1872, a new, better quality was introduced. Nevertheless, Civil War stocks were not exhausted until about 1880, and government parsimony dictated that the transition period lasted years, rather than the months originally intended (McChristian, 37–42).

Another problem was equipment designed in total ignorance of frontier conditions. Infantrymen, for example, were issued a packing system based on weight distribution that was superbly suited for

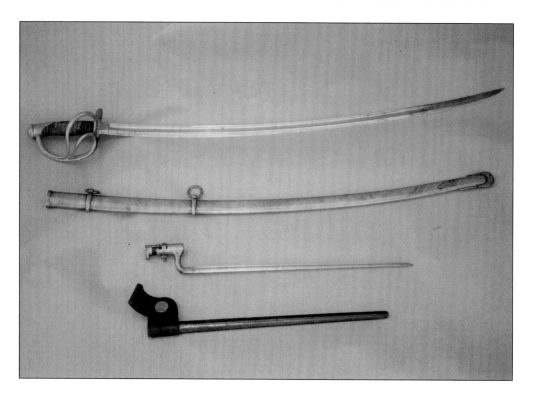

Useless accoutrements, the Model 1858 Cavalry saber and Model 1873 Infantry bayonet were regular issue during the Plains Wars, but were routinely left at post during field expeditions as they had no value in the hit-and-run fights with Native Americans. (Author's collection)

Europe and the American east. In the trackless expanses of the frontier, however, it only added a mass of additional field equipment that was an impediment for a foot soldier on a forced march. The average infantryman much preferred to roll up a few essentials in a blanket and sling it over his shoulder, with a haversack hanging down to one side. The army also insisted on cartridge boxes fastened to the waist-belt, a carry-over from the paper cartridge of muzzle-loading arms. The brass cartridge, however, made the box redundant, and soldiers often fashioned cartridge belts with loops on them, in the civilian style. Not until 1876, however, did the Bureau of Ordnance bow to reality, and issue a looped cartridge belt (McChristian, 178–79, 196–97; Utley, 1984, 75).

Cavalrymen were issued sabers, and infantrymen bayonets, but the nature of Native American warfare gave little opportunity to use them. They routinely were left on post as useless encumbrances more suited for guard duty or parade than combat (Utley, 1984, 76).

Given the myriad weapons used during the Civil War, the army made efforts to standardize. Not until 1873, however, was the goal realized for both cavalry and infantry. The sidearm was Colt's Model 1873 Single Action Army revolver in .45-caliber. The breechloading Model 1873 Springfield became the standard shoulder arm, in .45–70 long rifle for the infantry, and .45–55 carbine for the cavalry. Both the handgun and the shoulder arms had drawbacks. The Colt's cylinder, fixed in a one-piece frame, had to be rotated by hand each time a cartridge was ejected or inserted. The Springfield's single-shot hinged-block action made it effective at long ranges, but proved a hindrance in close-in fighting, especially as more Native Americans acquired Winchester or Henry repeating rifles (Utley, 1984, 70–72).

Bugle of the type used by troops in the Plains Wars during the second half of the 19th century. Native Americans, most notably the Kiowa chief Satanta, and the Cheyenne Dog Soldiers, also acquired bugles and, according to some contemporary accounts, learned to signal with military calls. This was not unique to the American Plains; during the siege of Khartoum in 1885, Major Gen. C.G. Gordon reported that Sudanese Madhists used Egyptian Army bugle calls to confuse and demoralize troops defending the city. (Author's collection)

Regardless of weaponry, marksmanship was at best indifferent, because the government begrudged money spent on ammunition for target practice. Indeed, many soldiers went into combat totally unfamiliar with their firearms. Only after the Custer disaster of 1876, and the heavy losses at Bear Paw Mountain during the Nez Percé War a year later, was a regular program of marksmanship enforced (Rickey, 100–12).

Wars handed down through generations

With the end of the Seven Years' War, France ceded Louisiana west of the Mississippi to Spain, removing the threat of French intervention on the Spanish frontier. The most serious danger in the north now became the Plains Native Americans, and this dictated a reorganization of Spanish defenses. In 1767, the Marqués de Rubí, a professional soldier and diplomat, inspected the northern provinces to consider improvements to frontier defense. On his recommendation, most of the presidios north of the Rio Grande, including the long-suffering San Luis de las Amarillas on the San Sabá, were closed. A new line of defense would follow the Rio Grande up to about the 30th parallel, then across to the Pacific. The only presidios above the line would be Santa Fe, San Antonio, and Loreto (better known as La Bahia) at Goliad. The area of extreme eastern Texas would be managed out of New Orleans (Jackson, 72, 79–81).

Although Rubí's policy made the line of defense more workable, depredations by the Lipan Apaches continued. In 1781, faced with increasing raids, Colonel Juan de Ugalde, governor of Coahuila, began a series of punitive expeditions that damaged, but did not stop, the Apaches. In 1785, with his authority expanded, he initiated a new, devastating campaign that forced the Lipans and their Mescalero Apache allies to cut back their raids. Finally, in 1789, he moved deep into central Texas, establishing headquarters in the old, abandoned presidio on the San Sabá. On January 9, 1790, he surprised a large Native American camp on the Sabinal River, killing nearly 40, and capturing women, children, and the Apache livestock herds. In honor of the victory, a nearby canyon was named Cañon de Ugalde, which the Texans render as Uvalde Canyon (Weddle, 188–89).

After Ugalde's campaigns, an uneasy calm settled on the frontier. Aside from occasional raids against the settlements, the Native Americans generally stayed out on the plains. In 1821, however, a new people began arriving, first in small groups, but within a few years numbering into the thousands. In the spring of that year, in the final months of colonial rule, the Spanish government granted Moses Austin the right to bring American colonists into the Brazos and Colorado river valleys. Within months, Austin was dead, and Mexico had become independent, but the new government reaffirmed the agreement with his son, Stephen F. Austin.

As the American settlers moved into the Texas interior, the Plains tribes began raiding their livestock. The settlers retaliated and soon the friction degenerated into bloodshed. In response to the settlers' pleas for assistance, the Mexican governor in San Antonio authorized them to establish a local militia. On May 5, 1823, the first company was organized—the birth of the Texas Rangers (Barton, 61–62; Barker, 1:672).

For the next 13 years, Native Americans and Texas settlers raided and counterraided. But as the 1820s drew to a close and the 1830s began, the most serious problem was deteriorating relations with the Mexican government. During the War of Independence in 1835–36, Rangers protected the frontier, allowing the army to concentrate on the struggle with Mexico. After independence, the Rangers functioned as needed, sometimes as frontier minutemen, called up to handle a crisis and returning to their homes when finished, and sometimes as a volunteer militia, called up for specific lengths of service.

The Mexican army had scarcely evacuated Texas when the new republic suffered one of its worst Native American raids, very similar to what had occurred at the San Sabá Mission 78 years earlier. The scene was Parker's Fort, a stockaded settlement in east central Texas, where the forests of the east begin to give way to the plains. It was a religious community consisting of 21 adults and 13 children, many of whom were related to the Reverend James W. Parker, the leader. On May 19, 1836, most of the men were out working in the fields, and the gates of the stockade were open to admit the breeze. A band of about 500 Comanches and allies approached the settlement under a flag of truce. Upon reaching the gate, they rushed in. The fort was plundered. Five were killed, and five others were captured.

Eventually, the captives were ransomed except James Parker's niece, Cynthia Ann, and nephew, John, who were children at the time. John was raised as a warrior, and eventually moved to Mexico. Cynthia Ann was recovered in 1860, after 24 years captivity. She now was 33 years old, and remembered little of her former life besides her name. She existed as a virtual prisoner with her relatives. She left behind a son, Quanah Parker, the last great Comanche war chief (Plummer, 322ff.).

The raid on Parker's Fort inaugurated depredations that lasted the remainder of the decade. The Comanches destroyed isolated farms and ranches, and carried large numbers of women and children into captivity. In January 1840, they proposed a peace council, and the Texas government agreed provided they brought their captives to San Antonio as a pledge of good faith.

The Comanche delegation appeared on March 19, but brought only one captive, 15-year-old Matilda Lockhart, who carried the scars of intensive torture during her two years with the Native Americans. Twelve principal chiefs were taken into the old Spanish government house, while the others remained in the courtyard. Matilda told the government representatives that the Comanches planned to bring in the other captives one or two at a time in hopes of obtaining large ransoms. Troops then surrounded the building, and the Native Americans were told they would remain hostages until all captives were returned.

The chiefs drew their weapons, one stabbed a sentry, and the troops opened fire. When the fighting ended, 30 chiefs and warriors were dead, together with three women and two children. Twenty-seven women and children, and two old men were taken prisoner, while seven soldiers and citizens were killed, and eight wounded (Winfrey and Day, 1:101–2, 105–06; Brice, 22–25).

For months, the Comanches and their Kiowa allies held off retaliation, encouraged by Mexican agents to wait until the Texans had become complacent. Then, in early August, they swept across Texas, striking the little seaport town of Linnville on August 8. Some citizens were killed or captured, but most managed to escape to a steamer anchored in the harbor, where they watched the Native Americans plunder the warehouses (Brice, 28–33).

Elsewhere, Ranger companies and regular troops came together and, guided by Tonkawa Native American scouts, intercepted the Comanches at Plum Creek on August 12. Ranger Robert Hall noted they were decked out in plunder from Linnville. "Many of them put on cloth coats and buttoned them behind," Hall remembered. "Most of them had on stolen shoes and hats. They spread the calico over their horses and tied hundreds of yards of ribbon in their horses' manes and to their tails." The Texans dismounted and opened fire. The second volley disorganized the Comanches, and the Texans charged in, routing them ("Brazos," 53–55).

One participant in the Plum Creek fight was a young ranger named Jack Hays who, four years later, gave the Native Americans their rudest shock of the era. Accustomed to single-shot muzzle-loading rifles and pistols, a band of Comanches attempted to ambush Hays and his rangers west of Austin on June 8, 1844. Instead, they ran into five-shot Colt revolvers, their first encounter with repeating weapons. About 30 warriors had been killed and wounded when they fell back (Robinson, 2000, 70–71).

A year later, the United States annexed the Republic of Texas. American jurisdiction would

LEFT Parker's Fort, reconstructed on the original site for the Texas Centennial in 1936, shows the type of dwellings used by settlers who "forted up" for defense. A stockade forms the rear wall of the cabins. (Author's collection)

become official on February 19, 1846. From that point onward, the US government would be responsible for defending the Texans against the Plains Native Americans. Whether the US was capable of doing so was another matter.

The Northern Plains

While the Texans battled Native Americans on the Southern Plains, more and more emigrants followed the Platte valley in their trek toward Oregon and California. In 1843, close to 1,000 men, women, and children passed a fur-trading post, known locally as Fort Laramie, near the confluence of the Laramie and North Platte rivers in what is now eastern Wyoming (Lavender, 48). To ascertain that emigrants could travel

unmolested, the government sent Colonel Stephen Watts Kearny with 250 dragoons to meet with the Native Americans in the vicinity. On June 16, 1845, Kearny held a council with about 1,200 Native Americans near Fort Laramie, explaining to them the meaning behind the white movement.

I am opening a road for your white brethren. They are now following after me, and are journeying to the other side of the great mountains. They take with them their women, their children, and their cattle. They all go to bury their bones there, and never to return. You must not disturb them in their persons, or molest their property; neither must you on any account obstruct the road which I have now opened for them. Should you do so, your great father would be angry with you, and cause you to be punished.

No punitive action would be taken against the Native Americans for past depredations and killings, Kearny said, but he expected them to cease immediately.

The Native Americans listened politely, and pledged friendship. Kearny distributed gifts, and then, to further impress them with the government's power, he ordered several rounds fired from howitzers. The traders at the post told Kearny that until his visit, the Native Americans believed that the only white people were emigrants. The arrival of the soldiers with their artillery, however, created fear and uncertainty (Carleton, 246–50). And while this may have had the desired effect of convincing some to acquiesce, it may have made others all the more determined to resist.

In 1846, Congress passed a bill authorizing the construction of military posts to protect the road to Oregon. The first of these, Fort Kearny, Nebraska, was established two years later, and in 1849, the War Department purchased Fort Laramie for $4,000. Work began immediately to expand

This view of Fort Laramie, Wyoming, shows the open layout of most Western military posts, which actually were cantonments rather than fortified installations. (Little Bighorn Battlefield National Monument)

the post out in front of the old traders' stockade (Lavender, 52–53, 57–59).

Meanwhile, the westward movement gained impetus. Besides the on-going trek to Oregon, the discovery of gold in California and the development of Utah by the Mormons added to the numbers coming up the Platte. In order to maintain peace, the government decided to issue annuities in the form of food and merchandize to the Native Americans in exchange for their good behavior. An ancillary plan called for tools, farming equipment, and education, in hopes of turning the Native Americans into (by white standards at least) productive citizens. The annuity issue was a major event, bringing thousands of Native Americans to the vicinity. The first attempt to implement this program with the northern tribes was a treaty signed at Fort Laramie in 1851. The government, however, labored upon the erroneous assumption that Plains society functioned like white society and that a treaty signed by the chiefs was binding on the tribe itself. Having failed to realize how little actual control the chiefs had over individuals and events, the government erred again, by not providing sufficient military force to impose the peace in exchange for annuities. The following year, some 60,000 people in perhaps 12,000 wagons passed Fort Laramie. Given the Native American weakness for white livestock, a major confrontation was only a matter of time (Lavender, 48, 69ff.).

The breaking point came on August 18, 1854, when, after a series of attacks on emigrants during recent weeks, the Native Americans were congregated in the vicinity of Fort Laramie for their annuities. A Mormon wagon train was moving toward the fort, and as it passed one of the Sioux camps, a warrior named High Forehead killed and butchered one of the oxen, driving off its owner. Realizing this could mean trouble, the paramount chief, Brave Bear, went to Fort Laramie and suggested waiting a few days until the agent arrived to sort the matter out. The officers of the post, however, believed that if nothing was done the Native Americans would get completely out of hand. The following day, Lieutenant John L. Grattan, a brash young officer fresh from West Point, took 29 soldiers, an interpreter, and two pieces of artillery to the Native American camps, to demand the surrender of High Forehead. When Brave Bear offered restitution, Grattan refused. High Forehead, meanwhile, had armed himself and, like Grattan, was ready to fight. After about 45 minutes, Grattan ran out of patience and ordered his men to open fire. Brave Bear was mortally wounded, but others began to fight back. Then several hundred mounted warriors charged, and Grattan's command was cut to pieces. Only one soldier survived, and he died shortly afterwards (Hyde, 1987b, 56ff.).

Although a calm descended on the area around Fort Laramie after the fight, a call went up in the east for retribution. Secretary of War Jefferson Davis believed the incident had been deliberately planned by the Native Americans in order to plunder the annuity stores. He ordered Brigadier General William Harney to organize a retaliatory campaign. The quarter-century of bloodshed collectively known as the Sioux Wars had begun (Utley and Washburn, 205).

Battle on the Plains

The Southern Plains, 1845–61

The US Army's first serious encounter with Comanches came when it was more preoccupied with the Mexican War than with Native Americans. The army was consolidating along the Rio Grande for a push into the Mexican interior when, on July 22, 1846, a runner came to the occupied town of Camargo with word that a band was raiding along the river. They were burning ranches, killing men, carrying off women and livestock, and had already attacked a Texas Ranger camp three miles away. A detachment of rangers under Captain Ben McCulloch spent several days tracking them down throughout the vicinity, and passing ranches that had been raided. He failed to overtake them, however, and they continued their depredations beyond the reach of the US troops (Robinson, 2000, 84–85).

Military posts constructed in Texas after the Mexican War were virtually useless because they were garrisoned by infantry, and the outbreak of depredations in 1848 prompted the Texas government to form new companies of mounted rangers. Within a year, however, the state had exhausted its own financial resources, and the US government agreed to defray expenses. Occasionally the army went so far as to request the state muster Ranger companies to serve with US regular troops. Rarely, however, did the federal government reimburse the state (Robinson, 2000, Chapter 7).

In 1853, federal officials called a meeting with the leaders of the major Southern Plains tribes at Fort Atkinson, Kansas (a different Fort Atkinson from the one mentioned in the Arikara War), in an effort to end the raiding. The government insisted on the right to establish roads and military posts in the Native Americans' country, and demanded the return of captives. In exchange, the Native Americans would receive $18,000 in annual annuities for 10 years, with an option for a five-year renewal. The Native Americans resented the roads and military posts, and would not discuss captives. In the end, the most the government could get was a promise that there would be no future raids for livestock or captives. They had no intention, however, of honoring this pledge or returning the existing captives, and within a year they denied making any pledges (Mooney, 173–74).

Although Native Americans raided all along the Texas frontier line, the most serious depredations were in the north-west, along the upper Brazos and Trinity rivers. The state established two reservations in the upper Brazos country near the military posts of Fort Belknap and Camp Cooper, and while the Native Americans on the reservation generally were peaceful, the reserves were used as a haven by marauding bands. White settlers failed to distinguish between friendly and hostile, and took revenge where they could find it, raiding the reservations and murdering agency Native Americans. This brought retaliatory raids, and some Comanches from Camp Cooper actively participated in general depredations. Ultimately, the state closed the reservations and relocated those tribes to the Native American Territory. Nevertheless, raiding continued unabated, with atrocities committed by both sides (Robinson, 2000, Chapter 7).

The Northern Plains, 1854–61

After the Grattan fight, some Brulés wanted to avenge the death of Brave Bear. In November 1854, one group attacked a mail wagon below Fort Laramie, killing three people, while another raided a trading post west of the fort. Winter was relatively peaceful, but the Brulés

The Battle of Washita, November 27, 1868

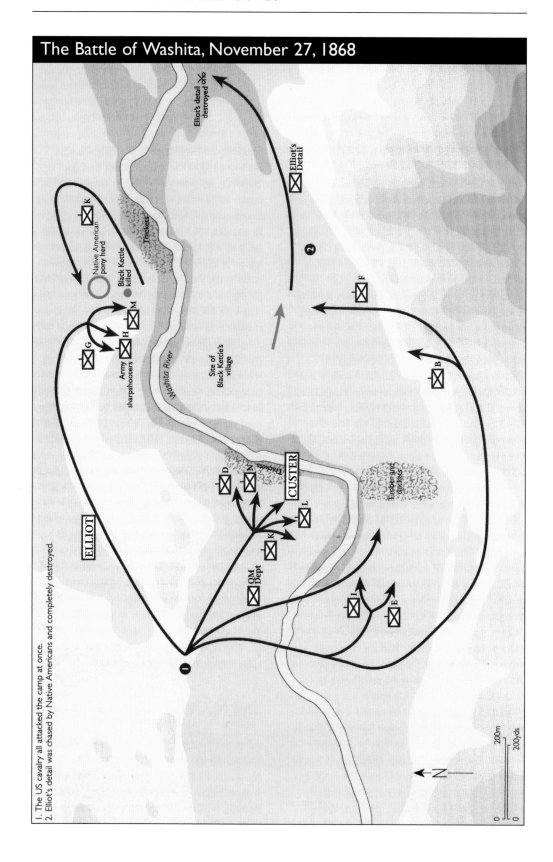

1. The US cavalry all attacked the camp at once.
2. Elliot's detail was chased by Native Americans and completely destroyed.

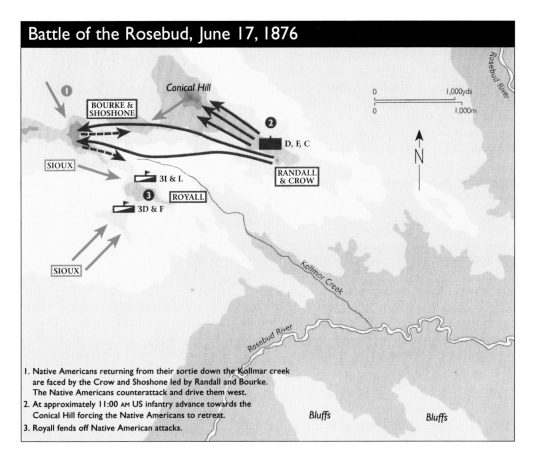

Battle of the Rosebud, June 17, 1876

Conical Hill

BOURKE & SHOSHONE

SIOUX

D, F, C

RANDALL & CROW

3I & L

ROYALL

3D & F

SIOUX

0   1,000yds

0   1,000m

N

Kollmar Creek

Rosebud River

Bluffs   Bluffs

1. Native Americans returning from their sortie down the Kollmar creek are faced by the Crow and Shoshone led by Randall and Bourke. The Native Americans counterattack and drive them west.
2. At approximately 11:00 AM US infantry advance towards the Conical Hill forcing the Native Americans to retreat.
3. Royall fends off Native American attacks.

resumed their depredations again in the spring of 1855. The possibility loomed that the outbreak might spread to other tribes and bands, so the large freight companies that used the Platte road lobbied in Washington for some sort of decisive action.

In August, Thomas Twiss, a former army officer, assumed the agency at Fort Laramie for the specific purpose of coordinating with the military, and Brigadier General W.S. Harney was ordered to organize an expedition. Twiss ordered all Native Americans who wished to avoid trouble to remain south of the North Platte river, where they would find sanctuary. Despite his efforts, some Native Americans refused to move south, and at dawn on September 3, Harney's infantry attacked a major Brulé camp under Little Thunder, near Ash Hollow, a few miles above the North Platte. Eighty-six people were killed, and 70 women and children were captured.

Harney then moved on to Fort Laramie, where he reassured the Native Americans who had accepted Twiss sanctuary. From there, he marched east to Fort Pierre, in what is now South Dakota, demonstrating that he could pass through the heart of Lakota country with impunity. At Pierre, the following spring, he bullied the chiefs into accepting government authority, and with the Platte road now apparently safe, the expedition was disbanded (Hyde, 1987a, 76–81).

The withdrawal of troops was premature. The Lakotas were humiliated by troops passing through their country, and even more by the treatment of their chiefs at Fort Pierre. They were also aware that, as settlers advanced into the Lower Missouri country, the Native Americans were being expelled, and realized that if this advance up the river continued, they could be next. From that point onward, the Lakota policy became one of war (1987a, 81–84).

The civil war

The federal government's failure to protect the frontier was one factor in Texas' decision to leave the Union in February 1861. Had the state chosen to reestablish itself as a sovereign republic, it might have succeeded. However, it opted to join the Confederate States of America which, within two months, became embroiled in a war to establish its independence from the United States. This war occupied the Confederate government's full attention, and it could spare no troops for frontier defense. In the meantime, federal troops—perhaps one-third of the entire strength of the US Army—were ordered to abandon their posts in Texas and withdraw. Although state troops tried to assume the responsibility for the frontier, the Confederacy's wartime demands quickly superceded the needs of the state (Robinson, 2000, Chapter 9).

Texas was not the only frontier state exposed by the war. In August 1862, the four-year-old Union State of Minnesota became the scene of one of the worst uprisings in US history. The eastern, or Santee Sioux had been dissatisfied since 1851, when they were pressured into ceding 24 million acres to the government in exchange for two reservations in the Minnesota Valley—designated upper and lower—and annuities spread over a 50-year period. The next step came in 1858 when, in response to settlers clamoring for more land, the government negotiated purchase of an additional million acres at 30 cents an acre (around 4,046 m²; later reduced by half). In both the 1851 and 1858 treaties, Native American traders submitted claims that were deducted from payments. Agents were appointed under the patronage system, and enriched themselves at the expense of the Native Americans.

In 1861, the Native Americans' crops failed, and during the following winter, they grew hungry. They were also aware that the male white population of fighting age had been substantially reduced by the requirements of war. The breaking point came in the summer of 1862, when annuities payments and the

ration issue were delayed for a month by bureaucratic squabbling. The Native Americans grew increasingly hungry, but when Chief Little Crow demanded the traders extend credit, they refused. Trader Andrew J. Myrick went so far as to say, "If they are hungry, let them eat grass." That thoughtless remark was one remark too many (Carley, 1–6).

On August 17, four Native Americans from the Upper Reserve killed five settlers at Acton Township, then took refuge in the Lower Reserve. At first, the Lower Reserve Sioux were undecided, but during a council

Refugees from the upper Sioux Agency in Minnesota pause during their flight after the Native Americans rose up in 1862. The photograph was taken by Adrian J. Ebell, a member of the group. (Minnesota Historical Society)

at Little Crow's house, the talk turned more toward war. Against his own better judgment, Little Crow ultimately agreed to lead a rising to expel the whites from the Minnesota valley.

At sunrise the following morning, the Native Americans attacked the settlement at the Lower Agency. Twenty whites were killed, and 10 captured. Forty-seven managed to escape while the Native Americans plundered the warehouses. Among the dead was Andrew Myrick, whose body was found with his mouth stuffed with grass. The war spread up the valley to the Upper Agency, leaving a wake of death and destruction. A detachment sent from Fort Ridgely was ambushed with a loss of 24 men. At the Upper Agency, several leaders opposed the war, and one, John Other Day, moved the whites into the brick warehouse. At daybreak on August 19, he managed to get 62 refugees across the river to safety.

The Minnesota Uprising 1862

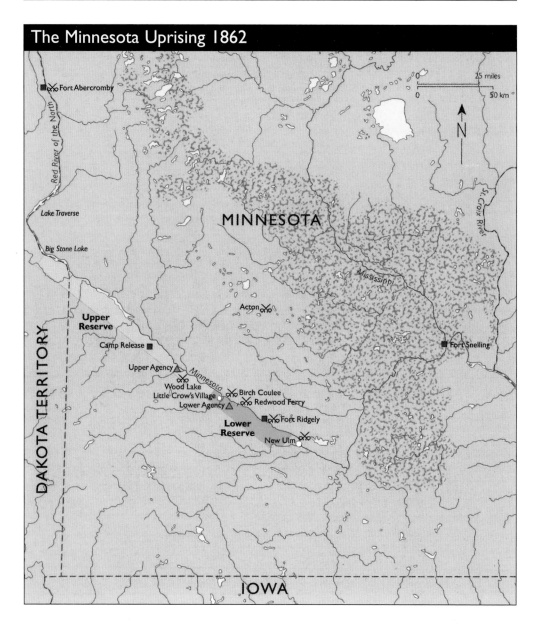

The Native Americans raged through the area destroying homesteads, killing, and carrying people into captivity. Refugees poured into Fort Ridgely, an open cantonment without defensive works, and a courier was sent for help. Both the fort and the town of New Ulm were attacked several times, but managed to hold with severe losses.

The failure to take Fort Ridgely and New Ulm was the turning point. Troops were dispatched to the area, along with citizen volunteers. The Native Americans were

defeated at Wood Lake on September 23, and three days later surrendered. Some 269 white and mixed-blood captives were released. Over the next six weeks, a military tribunal hastily tried 392 Native Americans for their part in the uprising, hearing as many as 40 cases in a single day. When it adjourned on November 5, 307 had been sentence to death, and 16 to prison. Brevet Major General John Pope, commander of the military division, commuted one death sentence to prison. As the condemned prisoners were marched through New Ulm en route to internment, troops had to protect them from angry mobs.

At the behest of Episcopal Bishop Henry Whipple, President Lincoln reviewed and commuted the death sentences of all but 39 prisoners who could be definitely established as having committed murder or rape. One of these was later reprieved because the testimony against him was questionable. The others were hanged in a mass execution in Mankato, Minnesota, on December 26. Two leaders of the rising who had fled into Canada later were kidnapped, spirited back to the United States, tried, and hanged. The hapless Little Crow fled into Dakota Territory, but returned a year later, and was killed by a farmer (Carley).

No one will ever know the exact number of soldiers and settlers killed in the rising. Estimates range from 450 to 800, but 500 seems to be a reasonable estimate. The Native Americans later indicated their losses in the actual fighting were about 21 (Carley, 1).

Several leaders besides Little Crow fled into the Dakotas, where they told their stories to the Plains Sioux. The latter, already angered by prospectors crowding through their territory en route to newly discovered Montana gold fields, were ready to listen. The situation was aggravated by military expeditions into the Dakotas led by Brigadier-Generals Henry Hastings Sibley and Alfred Sully. Sully campaigned as far as the Yellowstone river, pursuing not only fleeing Santees from Minnesota, but also the Lakotas through whose territory he marched. The final blow to their dignity came in July 1864, when Sully founded Fort Rice in what is now North Dakota, establishing a permanent military presence on the Upper Missouri. War spread across the Northern Plains (Utley and Washburn, 231–32).

Like the Santee Sioux in Minnesota, the Kiowas and Comanches of the Southern Plains were aware that trouble between the whites had caused a withdrawal of troops. Both Union and Confederacy tried to enlist the Native Americans in their cause. Confederate Brigadier General Albert Pike, who commanded the Department of the

Native American Territory, advised a group of Native Americans that he had "no objection" if they attacked federal wagon trains. "To go on the warpath somewhere else is the best way to keep them from troubling Texas," he explained to President Jefferson Davis (United States Department of War, *War of the Rebellion*, May 4, 1862, Series 1, 13:822). Federal officials, on the other hand, encouraged the Kiowas "to do all the damage they could to Texas ..." (Mooney, 179).

Being opportunists, the Kiowas and Comanches raided both sides. The Texas frontier was particularly vulnerable. Men were loath to enlist for Native American fighting when the Confederate government might conscript frontier defense units for the war in the East. Only when they were assured they would be exempt from the Confederate draft would they join Texas's Frontier Regiment, preferring to risk their lives for their homes rather than the Southern Cause. Although a smallpox epidemic among the Native Americans in 1862 gave the state a reprieve, the closing weeks of 1863 and the year of 1864 witnessed the worst depredations in Texas history.

The most devastating raid came on October 13, 1864, when several hundred Comanches and Kiowas swooped down on Young County, about 100 miles (160 km) west of Fort Worth. The settlers were completely surprised. Some were killed or captured, while others fled to the well-built home of a rancher named George Bragg, where they held off a six-hour siege. Still others reached the ranch too late, and hid in the brush along Elm Creek, listening to the fighting only a few yards away. By the time help arrived the next day, the Native Americans had retreated, leaving behind 11 dead settlers, and carrying with them seven women and children—white and black—as captives. They also took over 1,000 head of cattle (Hamby; United States Department of War, *War of the Rebellion*, Series 1, Vol. 41, 1:885–86). (Over the next year, all the captives were ransomed except an 18-month-old girl who was never seen again).

Thirty-eight Sioux involved in the rising are executed in a mass hanging at Mankato, Minnesota, on December 26, 1862. More than 300 were condemned, but President Abraham Lincoln commuted the sentences of all those not actually guilty of murder or rape. (Minnesota Historical Society)

The Native Americans took their captives to a group of winter camps situated along the Canadian river in northern Texas, near the ruins of an abandoned trading post called Adobe Walls. Once they had settled in, the younger warriors went out raiding again, this time moving into Colorado and New Mexico. At Adobe Walls, however, they were exposed to attack by troops from Union-held forts in New Mexico. On November 24, Native American scouts attached to the First New Mexico Volunteer Cavalry located the camps, and informed their commander, Colonel Christopher (Kit) Carson, one of the era's greatest frontiersmen. After a night march, Carson's troops overran the westernmost camp, occupied by the Kiowas, shortly after 8:00 AM the next day.

The warriors gave ground slowly over the 4 miles (6.5 km) between their camp and the ruins. At Adobe Walls, however,

they turned and made a stand. Finally, a pair of mountain howitzers was brought up, and the Native Americans were driven out. Carson halted at the ruins to rest and feed his men. Downriver, Dohasen, the aging paramount chief of the Kiowas, managed to round up about 1,000 warriors from the main camp, who rode back and attacked. After fierce fighting, the howitzers opened up with explosive shells, and the Native Americans abandoned the field. Carson destroyed about 150 lodges, with stores and munitions. Believing it unsafe to remain in the area, he withdrew back to New Mexico, unaware of the recent Young County raid, or that the captives had been driven into the brush and hidden when the fighting started (United States department of War, *War of the Rebellion*, Series 1, Vol. 41, 1:842; Mooney, 315–17).

The cumulative raiding elsewhere frightened the citizens of Colorado. Most of the tribes in the vicinity admitted that the Lakotas were trying to unite them into attacking travelers on the Platte and Arkansas roads, and the local Cheyennes were restless. Territorial Govenor John Evans hoped to negotiate a new treaty placing them on a reservation, but they refused, saying they had been swindled out of enough land. Evans, who was looking for an excuse to seize what he could not obtain by treaty, was ready to believe that the Cheyennes were plotting with the Lakotas to clear the region of whites. Colonel John M. Chivington, commander of the Military District of Colorado, was prepared to agree. The Cheyennes themselves were divided. The militant Dog Soldier Society wanted war, but so far, a group of peace chiefs headed by Black Kettle maintained the upper hand (Hoig, 1961, 31–34).

In spring 1864, Native Americans ran off some cattle, and troops were ordered out on punitive expeditions. On April 12, they clashed with a small band of Cheyennes, setting a new war into motion. A few weeks later, soldiers attacked and destroyed a Cheyenne camp in a canyon near Cedar Bluffs. A third fight occurred on May 16, when a military detachment engaged Cheyennes about 3 miles (4.5 km) from the Smoky Hill river, and the well-known peace chief Lean Bear was killed.

The local raids, combined with regular reports of Lakota depredations along the Platte road, created a panic in Colorado. Native Americans were not the only threat. Two years earlier, a Confederate advance on the territory had been thrown back, but many feared another attempt. As much as anything else, however, was the underlying fear of a general uprising that would turn Colorado into another Minnesota. To counter the supposed threat, Evans raised a regiment of 100-day volunteers, the Third Colorado Cavalry (54–55).

Among the Cheyennes, Black Kettle and the peace faction were no longer able to restrain the Dog Soldiers or the young warriors from raiding. Soon Lakotas, Arapahos, Kiowas, and Comanches joined. Most of the depredations were in Kansas or southern Nebraska, but there was a real possibility of their spreading into Colorado. As winter approached, however, the peace faction began reasserting itself, and on

September 28, Black Kettle and other Cheyenne and Arapaho peace chiefs met with Evans and Chivington, and came away with the idea that if they settled in the vicinity of a military post, they would be safe. In November, Black Kettle and about 600 followers moved their camp to the Sand Creek valley, about 40 miles (65 km) from Fort Lyon. Relations with the soldiers were good, and Black Kettle assumed he was safe.

Elsewhere, however, the men of the Third Colorado, recruited from the lower echelons of society, were complaining that they would not have a chance to kill Native Americans before their enlistments expired. Chivington led them to Sand Creek where, on November 29, he deployed 700 men and four howitzers around the camp. Black Kettle ran up a US flag and a white flag over his tipi, but the soldiers charged. Chivington, who had remarked that he hoped to be "wading in gore," wanted no prisoners, and men, women, and children were killed indiscriminately. Black Kettle managed to escape, but some 200 – mostly women and children—were killed and mutilated. The Third Colorado returned triumphantly to Denver where 100 scalps were exhibited on the stage of the local theater (Hoig, 1961, United States Congress; Utley and Washburn, 234–35).

If the citizens of Denver were ready to greet Chivington as a conquering hero, others were not. Even in Colorado, there was enough outrage to reverberate to Washington, where the Joint Committee on the Conduct of the War launched an investigation. Although the committee's main purpose was to investigate the myriad blunders and accusations that arose from the Civil War, any military action during that period, including fighting Native Americans, was subject to inquiry. The final report assigned varying degrees of blame, but singled out one special villain. Chivington, the report said, wearing the uniform of the United States and with the honor of the nation in his trust, "deliberately planned and executed a foul and dastardly massacre which would have disgraced the veriest savage among those who were the victims of his cruelty." It concluded "for the purpose of vindicating the cause of justice and upholding the honor of the nation, prompt and energetic measures should be at once taken to remove from office those who have thus disgraced the government ... and to punish, as their crimes deserve, those who have been guilty of these brutal and cowardly acts." Due to a legal technicality, however, Chivington could only be censured, and no one ever came to trial (Hoig, *1961*, 165–69; United States Congress, V–VI).

Repercussions spread across the plains. The Southern tribes burned for revenge, and the Northern tribes were still smoldering over their conflicts with Sibley and Sully. Native Americans devastated the Platte valley, and on July 26, 1865, hundreds of warriors fell on the military post at the Upper Platte bridge, severely beating a cavalry detachment, and wiping out a supply train. In response, Sully and Brevet Major General Patrick E. Connor mounted a two-pronged expedition. Sully took his troops into Dakota Territory with little result, but Connor met with more success in Wyoming, carrying the war deep into Lakota country. Eventually, however, the campaign failed because of distance from support, unfamiliarity with the terrain, bitterly cold weather, and food shortages. The government directed that henceforth, efforts should be directed at defending the roads (Utley and Washburn, 235).

The Southern Plains 1861–77

As the Civil War drew to a close, an uneasy calm settled on the Southern Plains. Kit Carson's fight at Adobe Walls had shaken the Native Americans, who were not accustomed to the military being able to reach so deep into their territory. They asked for peace and, in response, the government appointed a treaty commission to meet with the Native Americans at the mouth of the Little Arkansas river, at the present site of Wichita, Kansas, in mid-October 1865. Although the

Kiowas attended, many Plains tribes, including powerful elements of the Southern Cheyennes, boycotted the council because of suspicion and outrage stemming from the Sand Creek Massacre. By October 18, most of the leaders present signed (Mooney, 179–80).

The Kiowas agreed to a reservation south of the Arkansas river, with an agency at Fort Zarah, Kansas. Dohasen did much of the negotiating on their behalf, but it was increasingly obvious the old chief would not live much longer, and already factions were vying for leadership after his death. The main contenders were the powerful war chiefs Satanta and Lone Wolf. There was, however, a new contender, the younger chief Kicking Bird, who, although a valiant war leader, realized that the sheer demographic and technological superiority of the whites meant that they ultimately must prevail. Thus, while Satanta and Lone Wolf competed for leadership of the tribe as a whole, and the war faction in particular, Kicking Bird began forming a peace faction (Robinson, 1998, 43–44).

For the time being, at least, the Little Arkansas Treaty allowed travelers and freight to follow the Santa Fe Trail, the Smoky Hill road to Denver, and journey up the Platte without serious incident. Nevertheless, the region of the Smoky Hill and Republican rivers in western Kansas remained a trouble spot. The Cheyenne Dog Soldiers, who had boycotted the treaty council, resented the government's insistence that they give up their hunting grounds along the Smoky Hill. Even more ominous, the Red Cloud War, then being waged along the Bozeman Trail of Wyoming and Montana, was beginning to spill over into the Southern Plains. Already, there had been raids along the Republican river in Kansas, and the Cheyennes, though still peaceful, were restless. Major Henry Douglass, commander of Fort Dodge, advised his superior, Major General Winfield Scott Hancock, that large, well-armed bands of Sioux, Cheyennes, and Arapahos were moving south, and he expected trouble (Leckie, 30–33).

In April 1867, Hancock went to Fort Larned, Kansas, where he met with four

Red River War 1874–75

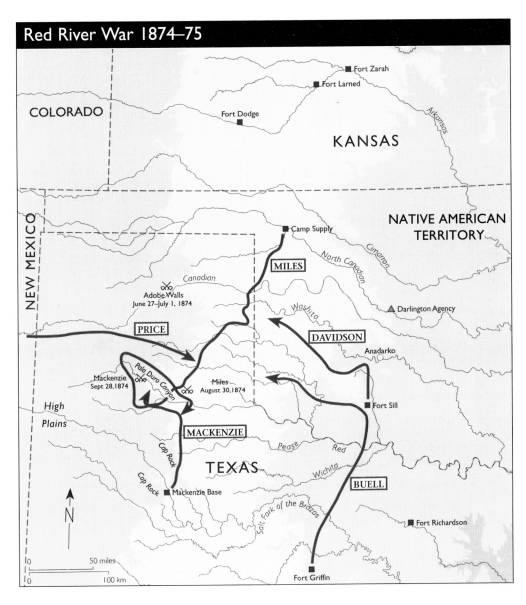

chiefs from a Cheyenne–Oglala camp about 30 miles (45 km) away. Failing to bully them into submission, he marched on the village on April 15. Fearing another massacre like Sand Creek, the Native Americans fled, and Lieutenant Colonel George Armstrong Custer took a cavalry detachment in pursuit. It was Custer's first Native American expedition. He noted depredations along the Smoky Hill road, and that many people had been killed. Although Hancock had no evidence the same Native Americans were involved, he ordered the camp destroyed (Hancock).

Now he sent Custer to seek out and destroy any hostile Native Americans, and Custer spent the first half of the summer chasing them to no avail. The only engagements of any real significance were an attack on his supply train, which was beaten back, and the complete destruction of a 10-man detail under Lieutenant Lyman S. Kidder. Ironically, Kidder and his men were wiped out by Oglalas under the chief Pawnee Killer, who had spent the spring and summer convincing Custer and Hancock of his good will.

Major General Winfield Scott Hancock's troops camp outside Fort Harker, Kansas, as they prepare for the first post-Civil War expedition against Southern Plains Native Americans in April 1867. The conflict, known as Hancock's War, proved farcical, and created more problems than it solved. (Kansas State Historical Society)

Hancock's War, as it came to be called, was the first concerted military action against Plains Native Americans after the Civil War. Its failure filled the various Sioux bands with contempt for the military, and convinced many erstwhile Cheyenne peace chiefs that they had no alternative but war (Robinson, 1993; Utley and Washburn, 241, 244).

The specter of new bloodshed in the wake of a bloody civil war prompted public pressure on the government to negotiate a solution.

On October 19, 1867, a treaty council convened between representatives of the federal government and leaders of the major Southern Plains tribes at Medicine Lodge, Kansas. The commissioners tried to impress on the Native Americans that the advance of white civilization meant they would have to give up their warrior/hunter way of life, settle down, and become assimilated.

In the end, the Native Americans grudgingly agreed to the treaty. The Kiowas and Comanches would settle on a reservation near what would become Fort Sill, Oklahoma; the Caddoes, Wichitas, and affiliated tribes about 60 miles (100 km) to the north at Anadarko; and the Southern Cheyennes and Arapahos farther north at what would become

Darlington. They would be allowed to hunt buffalo unmolested south of the Cimarron River, meanwhile establishing farms and permanent homes, and sending their children to government schools at the agencies. The government would provide rations to supplement the buffalo diet for an indefinite period until they were firmly established. How the government expected the Native Americans to make a 180-degree reversal of their ancient culture in only a few years was not explained (Robinson, 1998, Chapter 5).

Although many Native Americans attempted to congregate at the agencies, the government procrastinated in carrying out the treaty provisions. As the months passed, the Native Americans grew increasingly destitute

and restless. In early 1868, the Kiowas and Comanches began plundering into Texas. Hancock's successor, Major General Philip H. Sheridan, hoped to alleviate some of the problem by issuing rations from army supplies, but these were limited, and congress still procrastinated, not authorizing a Native American appropriation until late July. By then, it was too late. A Cheyenne war party attacked their ancient enemies, the Kaw Native Americans, and ransacked a few settlers' houses in the process. Throughout the remainder of the summer, clashes between Native Americans and whites accelerated.

Cavalry detachments patrolled the region of the Saline, Solomon, and Smoky Hill rivers with little results, although after one fight, a troops expedition recovered two captive women. Sheridan instructed his aide, Major George A. (Sandy) Forsyth, to take Lieutenant F.H. Beecher, nephew of the renowned minister Henry Ward Beecher, and 50 handpicked frontiersmen and look for the Native Americans. Forsyth departed Fort Hays, Kansas, on August 29. On the morning of September 17, the expedition suddenly found itself confronted by hundreds of Cheyennes and Oglalas. Forsyth led the men to a small island in the Arickaree River, where they entrenched among the low trees and bushes.

For seven days the whites held off a siege, eating horse meat and drinking water scooped from the sand, until the Native Americans departed and a relief column arrived from Fort Wallace. The fight subsequently became known as Beecher's Island, after the lieutenant, who was mortally wounded. Forsyth lost five others and 15 wounded who

One of the last photographs of Lieutenant Colonel George Armstrong Custer, taken in the spring of 1876, shows him with the shorter hair he preferred later in life. In the field, Custer tended to keep his hair cut close to his scalp for ease of cleanliness. (Author's collection)

recovered, including himself. The Native Americans lost at least 32 killed, including the great Cheyenne chief Roman Nose, and many more wounded (Leckie, Chapter 3).

Forsyth's fight, and a futile Native American hunting expedition by Sully, convinced Sheridan to wage a winter campaign, when lack of forage for their ponies would pen the Native Americans into winter camps in river valleys. He planned to drive the tribes onto their reservations, and kill any that held back. To command his cavalry, he retrieved Custer from Michigan, where he was whiling away an enforced suspension under sentence of court-martial.

The Kiowas and Comanches sensed that something was afoot, and began moving in toward the agency at Fort Cobb, in southwestern Oklahoma, which was declared a refuge for non-hostile bands. General Sherman, however, had declared all Cheyennes and Arapahos collectively hostile, regardless of whether or not they had actively participated in depredations. When Black Kettle and several other Cheyenne peace chiefs tried to bring their bands to Fort Cobb, they were told to camp elsewhere until notified otherwise (Leckie, 88–92; Hoig, 1976, 73–74).

On Sunday, November 22, 1868, the Seventh Cavalry marched out of the military depot of Camp Supply in heavy wind and snow, provisioned for 30 days in the field. Four days later, an advance party sent word that it was following a large Native American trail. By late November 27, scouts investigating the Washita River had found a Cheyenne camp under the hapless Black Kettle. The Seventh divided into four units, all of which hit camp simultaneously at dawn the following day. Within 10 minutes, the troops controlled the camp, and the warriors retreated among the trees and ravines to begin a return fire. The soldiers dismounted and moved against the Native American position for hand-to-hand fighting. This time, Black Kettle's luck ran out. He and his wife were killed as they crossed the river trying to escape. The fighting began to die down, and Major Joel Elliott took a detachment of 17 men to round up fleeing warriors (Hoig, 1976).

Custer's troops attack a Cheyenne village on the Washita river in Oklahoma in November 1868. Among the dead was the Cheyenne peace chief Black Kettle, who had survived the Sand Creek Massacre almost exactly four years earlier. (Author's collection)

About 10:00 AM, large numbers of Native Americans counterattacked, and Custer realized this was one of several major camps along the river. Pickets ran in saying they had been driven from their positions, and a patrol was driven back by Arapahos. In the distance, they heard gunfire, but did not realize that Elliott's detachment was being massacred. Late afternoon, Custer ordered a withdrawal without bothering to check on Elliott's situation. Not until December 10 were the bodies discovered. Although extensive mop-up operations remained, the Winter Campaign had proven itself, and ultimately the Southern Plains Native Americans were driven into their agencies (Hoig, 1976, 134–40; Leckie, 133).

When President Grant implemented his Peace Policy late the following year, the Native Americans initially appeared cooperative, but their interest was short-lived. Already, in the spring of 1869, raiding parties were slipping into Texas, and that year would prove to be

one of the bloodiest in the history of the state. In June, the Kiowas held their annual Sun Dance, which was attended by the Comanches, Kiowa-Apaches, and Southern Cheyennes. When it ended, raiders dispersed in all directions. The Cheyennes even attacked Camp Supply, and the Kiowas took 73 mules from the quartermaster's corral at newly established Fort Sill. In Texas, 15 people were killed in Jack County alone in a single month (Leckie, 136ff.).

The year 1870 was little better, and in 1871, the raiding began earlier than normal. On May 18 a band of about 150 Kiowas, Kiowa-Apaches, and Comanches attacked a wagon train carrying corn from Weatherford, Texas, to Fort Griffin. Seven teamsters were killed, and over 40 mules were driven off as plunder. (The incident is known to history as the Warren Wagon Train Massacre, after the owner of the train, freight contractor Henry Warren of Weatherford). When the survivors reached Fort Richardson that night, they were personally interviewed by General Sherman, who was on an inspection tour of Texas, and had passed over the same spot only a day earlier. He dispatched Colonel Ranald Mackenzie and a detachment of Fourth Cavalry to hunt down the Native Americans.

A fanciful woodcut shows the death of teamster Samuel Elliott during the Warren Wagon Train Massacre. In reality, Elliott was not tied to a wheel, but was strapped to a wagon tongue and roasted over a fire. (Author's collection)

Continuing on to Fort Sill, Sherman learned that the raiders, who were attached to the agency, had arrived almost simultaneously, and Satanta had boasted about it to Agent Lawrie Tatum, naming himself, the old chief Satank, Eagle Heart, and Big Tree as leaders. Tatum requested the Native Americans be arrested and sent to Texas for trial, and Sherman was happy to comply. Although Eagle Heart managed to slip away, the others were arrested, and turned over to Mackenzie, who had followed them to Sill. As the troops prepared the Native Americans for the trip to Texas, Satank jumped a guard and was killed. Satanta and Big Tree were confined at Fort Richardson, and tried for seven counts of murder in civil court in adjacent Jacksboro. They were sentenced to death, but Governor Edmund J. Davis, on advice of Tatum, commuted their sentences to life in prison as hostages for Kiowa good behavior (Robinson, 1997). This infuriated Sherman, who remarked, "Satanta ought to have been hung

and that would have ended the trouble …" (Quoted in Nye, 147).

Despite Tatum's hopes, the effect was only marginal. The Quahadi Comanches, under Cynthia Ann Parker's son, Quanah, continued to raid. Meanwhile, the imprisonment of Satanta and Big Tree had cost the Kiowa war faction prestige, and the war chiefs were out to regain it with new depredations. Although Mackenzie led campaigns during the summer and fall of 1871, he failed to suppress the Native Americans, and in 1872, the raids grew worse. In April, Kiowas attacked a wagon train at Howard's Wells in west Texas. Seventeen teamsters were killed, and the train was plundered (Nye, 152–54). On June 22, Mackenzie reported, "There have been more depredations lately than ever before—four murders in the last week that are really true and since [then], nine more reported, of the truth of which I am not yet convinced" (United States Department of War, Office of the Adjutant General, record group 391).

On September 29, however, Mackenzie captured a major Comanche camp on the North Fork of the Red River, destroying 262 lodges, and taking over 120 women, children,

Colonel Ranald S. Mackenzie was beset by bouts of insanity that eventually forced him out of the army. Nevertheless, he built the Fourth Cavalry into a first rate mobile assault force, and was victorious in both the Red River War and the Great Sioux War. (Author's collection)

Lone Wolf was one of the heads of the Kiowa war faction, and a leader in the Red River War of 1874–75. (Oklahoma State Historical Society)

and wounded as prisoners. They were interned at Fort Concho as hostages for the release of white captives. This was a shock for the Native Americans, who were not accustomed to having to bargain for the release of their own people. The raiding essentially ceased as they pondered their next move. The Kiowas, meanwhile, had settled down, because some of their chiefs had recently traveled to Washington and seen first hand the real power of the government. In consequence, the Friends Committee, the Quaker organization that supervised the agencies in Kansas and the Native American Territory, were advocating the release of Satanta and Big Tree as both reward and incentive to good behavior, and the Comanche captives became part of the bargain.

Eventually, the Fort Concho prisoners were released to their people. After some

argument, Govenor Davis agreed in 1873 to parole Satanta and Big Tree, subject to stringent conditions of enforcement by the federal government (Robinson, 1997).

Prison had taken much of the fight out of Satanta, and the much younger Big Tree had quickly grasped the reality of the situation. Even the militants, like Lone Wolf, had begun to settle. The Comanches, however, resumed raiding, and on November 30, James Haworth, who had succeeded Lawrie Tatum as agent, was told to withhold rations. The decision angered those who were not involved, and was made worse when the government rescinded the order. Contemptuous of the vacillation, the Comanches resumed their raiding, joined by young Kiowa warriors (Leckie, 181–82).

Even when issued, the rations were not adequate because the amounts had been predicated on the idea that the Native Americans would continue hunting buffalo for subsistence. In 1870, however, buffalo hides suddenly became valuable when a means was found to tan them for industrial leather. A skilled buffalo hunter could make substantially more than an eastern factory worker could, and in considerably less time, and soon the plains echoed with the booming of heavy-caliber rifles. Within three years, the buffalo were virtually exterminated north of the Cimarron River in Oklahoma, and the hide hunters moved south, deep into the Native American Territory and Texas, into the region that the Native Americans considered their exclusive hunting domain.

Besides buffalo, the Cheyennes and Arapahos were losing livestock to white horse and cattle thieves, who were raiding the herds and driving them into Kansas. Whiskey peddlers took advantage of the desperation, and alcoholism was becoming chronic. The breaking point came in May 1874, when

Hunters skin a buffalo near what is now Abilene, Texas, in 1874. The market for buffalo hides led to massive slaughter in the early 1870s, and was a major cause of the Red River War. (Texas State Library and Archives)

white raiders stole 43 ponies. A pursuit party of warriors attempted to recover them, but failing, ran off a herd of cattle near the Kansas line, where they clashed with federal cavalry. Fighting broke out in Kansas and the Native American Territory, and Native Americans began attacking buffalo hunters in northernmost Texas.

Raiding into Texas was increasingly dangerous. Mackenzie's highly mobile and skilled Fourth Cavalry had set the standard, and the departmental commander, Brigadier General Christopher C. Augur, kept scouting expeditions more or less constantly in the field. In his report for the period of September 30, 1873, to September 28, 1874, General Augur reported that although 60 citizens had been killed by Native Americans, 32 warriors were also known to have been killed, a heavy loss by Native American standards. Lone Wolf's son had been killed in one such raid, and the old war chief brooded over it throughout the winter and spring. On May 1, 1874, he joined a raiding party that went south to recover his son's body and devastate the Texas frontier (Leckie, 185ff.; Wallace, 103–04).

Among the normally secular, pragmatic Comanches, the desperation was such that a prophet appeared among their ranks for perhaps the only time in recorded history. His name was Isa-tai, and although a young man, barely out of his teens and unproven in battle, people were ready to believe his claim that he could vomit forth bullets by the wagon load. He had lost a favorite uncle during a raid in Texas, and burned for vengeance. Among his early converts was Quanah Parker. In May, Isa-tai organized a Sun Dance, common enough among other Plains tribes, but totally alien to Comanche culture. He used the gathering to reinforce his power as a messiah, and to whip up enthusiasm for war. Before the ritual was finished, Quanah had devised a plan that other chiefs approved. They would destroy a buffalo hunter settlement at Adobe Walls, near the site of Kit Carson's fight with the Kiowas 10 years earlier (Haley, 52–55).

At dawn on June 27, the Native Americans gathered on the ridges overlooking Adobe Walls, whose total population was 28 men and one woman, all hunters or suppliers. The men, however, had been up since 2:00 AM, shoring up the heavy sod roof of one of the buildings where they slept. Thus, when the Native Americans swept down, all but two managed to reach the safety of the buildings alive. The initial assault was driven back by the deadly fire of the hunters with their heavy buffalo rifles. The Native Americans then settled down for a siege, but by mid-afternoon, discouraged by mounting losses, they withdrew. Three hunters were killed, and 13 Native American bodies were found (Leckie, 191–93).

The Comanches and Cheyennes were ready for war, but to mount it on the scale they desired, they needed the Kiowas. Lone Wolf advocated war, but was opposed by Kicking Bird and the powerful peace faction. Many Kiowas waited to see which group would prevail. One by one, the leading chiefs and medicine men opted for peace, and the war faction collapsed. Kicking Bird led three-quarters of the Kiowa nation to Fort Sill to enroll as neutrals, leaving Lone Wolf and his supporters to do as they pleased (Robinson, 1997, 170–71).

Sheridan, who now commanded the Military Division of the Missouri encompassing the entire plains region, ordered five columns of troops to converge on the region where the hostiles were active. (Sheridan had been promoted to Lieutenant General in keeping with his new responsibilities). Colonel Nelson A. Miles would move south from Kansas with cavalry and infantry; Major William R. Price east from New Mexico with cavalry; Mackenzie northward, and Col. George Buell northwest into the high plains of Texas, with cavalry; and Lieutenant John W. Davidson west from Fort Sill. The Native Americans would be run down and battered back and forth between the military columns until subdued (Haley, 105).

At Darlington, little more than 10 percent of the Cheyennes remained on the reservation, and the situation was so tense

A self-made soldier, Colonel Nelson A. Miles was a martinet in his own right, but with little regard for the army and its formalities. In later life, he was the last general-in-chief of the army before the position was abolished in favor of an army chief of staff. (Little Bighorn Battlefield National Monument)

that the agent asked for military protection. A company arrived simultaneously with several bands of Comanches, and Lone Wolf's Kiowas were also known to be in the vicinity. The commander, Captain Gaines Lawson, requested reinforcements, and Colonel Davidson brought four companies of cavalry. Although the Comanches initially intended to surrender, Lone Wolf's

arrival initiated fighting, and eventually the Native Americans scattered out onto the plains (Leckie, 200–04).

From the north, Miles' infantry marched into Texas, where they struck a large Native American trail that led an advance unit into a Cheyenne ambush along Prairie Dog Fork of the Red River. When the main body of troops arrived, the Cheyennes broke and fled, and a

In 1863, a delegation of Southern Plains tribal leaders traveled to Washington, D.C., seeking a peace agreement. Lean Bear of the Cheyenne (front row, second from right) gave a speech asking for peace on both sides. (Library of Congress Prints and Photographs Division)

grounds that no Native American could have slipped past Miles. The mutilated bodies of the party were found later, prompting General Augur's acid comment, "A Commander against hostile Native Americans is never in such imminent danger as when fully satisfied that no Native Americans can possibly be near him" (Haley; quoted in Wallace, 81).

The Native Americans suffered one of their most crushing blows early September 28, when Mackenzie's cavalry, leading horses down a cliff-face in near darkness, attacked a string of winter camps in Palo Duro Canyon. Although most of the Native Americans managed to escape, the camps with their stores, and more than 1,000 captured ponies were destroyed. The Native Americans, now dismounted and destitute, slowly began drifting back to the agencies to surrender. Satanta turned himself in at Darlington on October 4. Although here is no evidence that he personally took part in any hostilities, he admitted to being at the Wichita Agency when fighting broke out, and had associated with hostile leaders. These were deemed parole violations, and he was returned to prison where he committed suicide four years later (Wallace, 124–27; Robinson, 1998, 188–92).

There was never any question of the outcome of the Red River War. Although the region was brutally hot, and water a constant issue (at one point Miles' men opened the veins of their arms to suck the blood and reduce the swelling of their tongues), the troops still had adequate mobility, along with overwhelming numerical superiority. Much of the region was heavily settled, and the soldiers were never critically far from support. There were few obstacles that the military could not overcome. The Native Americans, on the other hand, were never completely organized, and without the support of the majority of the

running fight ensued for about 20 miles (32 km) before the Native Americans managed to vanish among the canyons leading up to the high plains. Miles' presence in Texas, however, left too few troops to defend southern Kansas, and the Native Americans raided with virtual impunity. He was also overconfident. When a surveying party asked for military protection, it was refused on the

Kiowas, their fighting ability was limited. By June 2, 1875, when Quanah Parker's surrender officially ended the war, the leading chiefs had already been transported to Fort Marion, Florida, where they were interned for four years. Mop-up operations continued against small, isolated bands for another couple of years, but the 150-year conflict in the Southern Plains essentially had ended.

The Northern Plains 1861–77

The Northern Plains provided a totally different scenario. Much of the region was unsettled and, to a large extent, unknown. Military expeditions might range hundreds of miles from support. In winter, snow blocked travel over the open country, and in summer, temperatures could soar to over 100 degrees

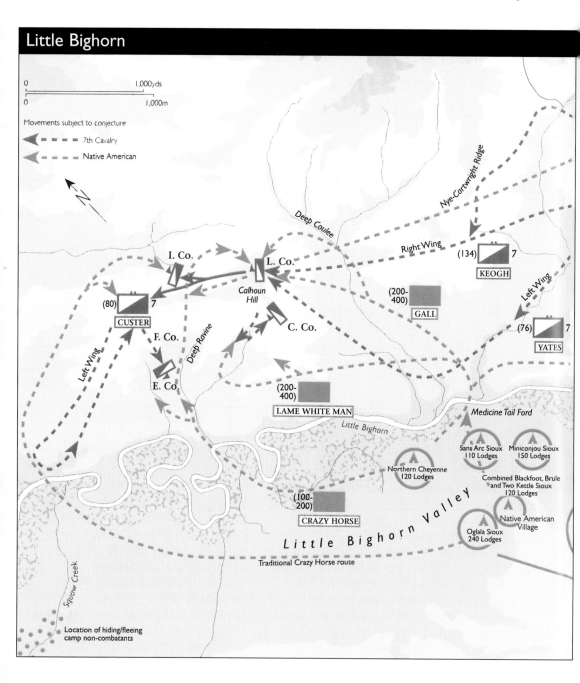

Little Bighorn

0   1,000 yds
0   1,000 m

Movements subject to conjecture

◀ ▬ ▬ ▬ ▬   7th Cavalry
◀ ▬ ▬ ▬ ▬   Native American

N

Deep Coulee

Nye-Cartwright Ridge

I. Co.   L. Co.   Right Wing   (134)   7   KEOGH

Calhoun Hill   (200–400)   GALL   Left Wing

(80)   7   CUSTER

F. Co.   Deep Ravine   C. Co.   (76)   7   YATES

Left Wing

E. Co.   (200–400)   LAME WHITE MAN

Little Bighorn   Medicine Tail Ford

Sans Arc Sioux   Miniconjou Sioux
110 Lodges   150 Lodges

Northern Cheyenne
120 Lodges   Combined Blackfoot, Brule and Two Kettle Sioux
120 Lodges

(100–200)   CRAZY HORSE   Native American Village

Oglala Sioux
240 Lodges

Little Bighorn Valley

Traditional Crazy Horse route

Squaw Creek

Location of hiding/fleeing camp non-combatants

Fahrenheit (38 degrees Celsius). The Native American tribes were powerful, militant, and, in the case of the Lakotas, could count their warriors in the thousands. It is significant that the greatest "massacres" of entire military units occurred in this region.

In 1865, while government commissioners negotiated what they thought were peace treaties with the Upper Missouri tribes, the bulk of the Lakota fighting power was in the Powder River country of Wyoming, celebrating its latest round of victories against the whites. In June 1866, their leaders finally appeared at Fort Laramie, but when they heard the government wanted roads across their country, they balked. A gold strike in western Montana in 1862 had led to the establishment of a government road, better known as the Bozeman Trail, from Fort Laramie to Montana, and the extensive

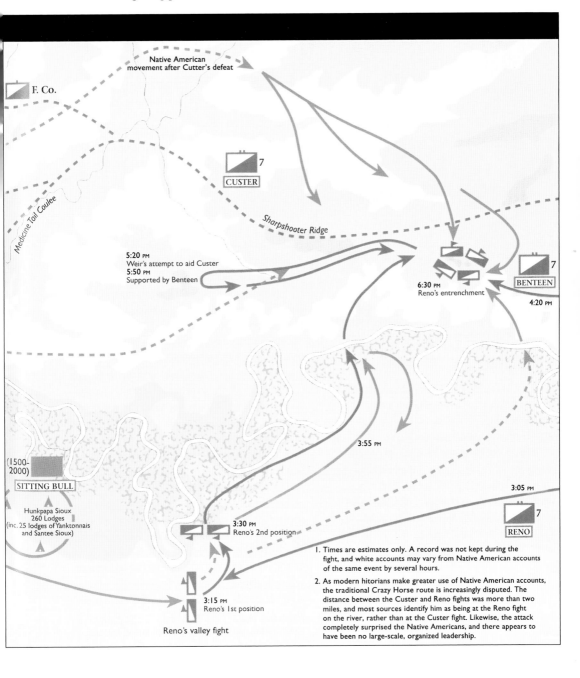

1. Times are estimates only. A record was not kept during the fight, and white accounts may vary from Native American accounts of the same event by several hours.

2. As modern hitorians make greater use of Native American accounts, the traditional Crazy Horse route is increasingly disputed. The distance between the Custer and Reno fights was more than two miles, and most sources identify him as being at the Reno fight on the river, rather than at the Custer fight. Likewise, the attack completely surprised the Native Americans, and there appears to have been no large-scale, organized leadership.

The Oglala chief Red Cloud fought the government to stand during the Red Cloud War of 1866–68. Although he sympathized with the hostilities during the subsequent Great Sioux War, he stayed out of the conflict. He remained a powerful force among the Lakota Sioux until his death in 1909. (Little Bighorn Battlefield National Monument)

travel on that road was a sore point. Not only were they determined to keep any new roads from being built, they also wanted the Bozeman closed. At a critical moment, a large number of new troops appeared, and the influential chiefs Red Cloud and Man Afraid of His Horses, suspecting a trick, departed with their followers. Discussions with the hostile Lakota bands collapsed (Hyde, 1987a, 137–39).

The arrival of these troops was nothing more than unlucky coincidence. Their leader, Colonel Henry B. Carrington, had been appointed commander of a military district to guard the Bozeman Trail. With his troops, he was to garrison General Connor's post of Fort

Reno, and construct two new forts, designated as Phil Kearny and C.F. Smith, farther up the trail. It was a sign of the government's post-Civil War economy that Carrington had only 700 infantrymen and a handful of cavalry to maintain order in a region where Connor had been given 3,000 cavalry.

Red Cloud was determined not to allow the military into the area. On July 17, 1866, Native Americans infiltrated a picket line at the Fort Phil Kearny construction site, and stampeded the horses. Luring a pursuit party beyond immediate support, they turned on it, and the soldiers barely escaped annihilation. En route back to the fort, they came upon a trader's wagon with six dead and mutilated white men. This inaugurated what became known to history as the Red Cloud War (Hyde, 1987a, 139–40; Brown, 77–78).

Throughout the summer and fall, Carrington sent messages to his superiors asking for cavalry. Meanwhile, depredations continued and the cemetery at Fort Phil Kearny began to fill even as the buildings were being constructed. Red Cloud had rallied his own Oglalas, together with Hunkapaps, Brulés, Miniconjous, Cheyennes, Arapahos, and Gros Ventres.

On November 3, cavalrymen arrived, among them Captain William J. Fetterman, an ambitious young officer with an enviable combat record in the Civil War. Like many such officers, however, he was contemptuous of Native Americans, and bragged that with 80 men he could subdue the entire Sioux nation.

For defensive purposes, Fort Phil Kearny was built on an open plain. Wood for construction was provided from a heavily guarded saw mill several miles away. The most vulnerable point was the wood train carrying lumber to the fort from the mill. The train had been attacked several times, and Carrington determined that the Native Americans hoped to lead a relief column away from support and massacre it. On December 21, the train again was attacked. Fetterman demanded that he lead the relief column, and Carrington ordered him to rescue the train and return immediately. Instead, Fetterman chased the Native Americans several miles

beyond a line of hills. There, he found himself surrounded by masses of warriors who massacred the entire column. By coincidence, it consisted of 80 men (Brown).

The Red Cloud War lasted another 18 months. Again, however, the government was unwilling to undertake a major Native American campaign so close to the end of the Civil War. Consequently, a treaty commission met with Red Cloud and other chiefs at Fort Laramie in 1868, and negotiated a treaty that effectively ended the Sioux Wars for the time being. The Native Americans were given a massive reservation encompassing the entire western half of the modern state of South Dakota, including the Black Hills. Northeastern Wyoming and southeastern Montana were designated unceded Native American lands off the reservation, where they might roam as they pleased. Except for necessary government military, civil, and scientific expeditions, no outsider would be permitted on the reservation or the unceded lands without joint permission of the Native Americans and the government. The Bozeman Trail would be closed, and Forts

Members of the Fort Laramie Treaty Commission pose with a Lakota woman during negotiations in 1868. Among the key members were (from left to left center), Brigadier General Alfred H. Terry, commander of the Department of Dakota; Brigadier General William Harney, an experienced Plains Native American fighter; and Lieutenant General W. T. Sherman who, the following year, became general-in-chief of the army. (Little Bighorn Battlefield National Monument)

Reno, Phil Kearny, and C.F. Smith would be abandoned. Finally, the government would provide annuities, rations, job training, and schools (DeLand, 15:125–27; Lazarus, 433ff.).

For a while, the treaty appeared workable. However, the completion of the first transcontinental railroad in 1869 opened up the plains, and initiated a railroad construction boom. Other lines began moving across the region, through Kansas and the Dakotas, stirring resentment among the tribes. Surveying crews laying out the routes required military protection. Rations and annuities were often late, and the Native Americans on the reservation began to suffer. Resistance centered around the Hunkpapa chief Sitting Bull, who

Custer's two-mile (3 km) wagon train passes through Castle Creek Valley during the 1874 Black Hills Expedition. Custer confirmed the existence of gold in the hills, initiating a rush that led to the Great Sioux War of 1875–76. (Little Bighorn Battlefield National Monument)

refused to accept the treaty, and remained in the unceded lands, encouraging others to leave the reservation and join him.

In 1874, Custer led a surveying expedition into the Black Hills that confirmed the existence of gold. This information arrived in the east at a time of severe economic depression, and soon the hills were flooded with miners and prospectors. This was in clear violation of the Fort Laramie Treaty, and when the military proved inadequate for the task of eviction, the Native Americans took matters

their reservations on or before January 31, 1876, or be declared hostile. The deadline came and went, and on February 1, the matter was turned over to the War Department.

General Sheridan believed that a winter campaign involving a three-pronged attack, similar to the tactics on the Southern Plains, would be effective against the Northern tribes. Accordingly, he notified the two generals in whose jurisdictions the war would be waged, Crook in the Department of the Platte in Omaha, Nebraska, and Alfred Terry of the Department of Dakota in St. Paul, Minnesota. A column of Crook's troops would move north from Wyoming, while one column of Terry's would move east from western Montana, and a second column from Terry would move west from Dakota. The three columns would batter the Native Americans back and forth between them, and force them onto the reservations. Colonel John Gibbon was designated to lead the Montana column, while Custer would lead the Dakota column. Crook would make his own arrangements, but given his preference for field service, it was presumed he would have a heavier hand in the Wyoming column than Terry would have in his.

Unfamiliar with the northern climate, Sheridan did not realize until too late that it would be well into spring before either Gibbon or Custer could move. Crook, meanwhile, went to Wyoming, where he began to organize his troops. Nominal command of the expedition fell to Colonel Joseph J. Reynolds, with Crook along as an "observer." Nevertheless, there was little question in anyone's mind that Crook was actually in charge, and this seriously undermined Reynolds' position.

The result was a fiasco. Reynolds attacked a village, which Crook insisted to his dying day belonged to Crazy Horse, but in fact was a Cheyenne village. The attack itself was bungled so badly that Crook, looking for scapegoats, court-martialed Reynolds and two other officers. The Cheyennes, who until now considered the war a Lakota problem, turned hostile. Together with Crazy Horse's Oglalas, they combined with Sitting Bull's Hunkpapas in a massive, constantly moving Native

into their own hands and began attacking the intruders. The government then attempted to buy the hills from the Native Americans, and failing that, to lease them. But when the Native Americans refused to agree to either, it became obvious the hills would have to be taken by force. On December 6, 1875, Native American agents were directed that all Native Americans would have to be within

American camp. In Montana, Gibbon's column finally got under way in late March. Twice his scouts found the giant camp and, each time, Gibbon did nothing. Not until May 17 did the Dakota column get moving, and then with General Terry in charge. Custer was relegated to a subordinate role, because earlier in the year, he had publicly humiliated President Grant, and only Terry's intervention saved his career.

On May 28, Crook took to the field again. Establishing a base camp at Goose Creek, in the foothills of the Bighorn Mountains, he hunted and fished, waiting for the Crow and Shoshone Native American scouts that finally joined him in mid-June. At 5:00 AM, June 16, the column moved north again (Robinson, 2001, Chapter 10). One officer, however, commented, "I did not think that General Crook knew where [the hostile Native Americans] were, and I did not think our

Last Stand Hill at Little Bighorn Battlefield National Monument is dotted with white government markers approximating where the bodies of Custer and his immediate command were found. The large shaft on the crest marks the mass grave of soldiers after they were removed from makeshift graves and reinterred. (Author's collection)

friendly Native Americans knew where they were, and no one conceived we would find them in the great force we did" (Mills, 398).

The next morning, during a break in the march for coffee along the Rosebud River, Crook's Native American scouts prowling the hills collided with hunters from the vast hostile camp that now was just a few miles away. Crook's scouts hurried back to the soldiers, followed by masses of hostiles. The ensuing battle lasted several hours, as the hostiles tried to draw the individual companies of soldiers into the hills, cut them off, and destroy them piecemeal. Finally, as their losses mounted, they broke off and returned to their camp, leaving Crook in possession of the battlefield, but so badly mauled that he had no choice but to withdraw back into Wyoming. Although he claimed victory until he died, in fact, he had barely averted disaster. The Native Americans, meanwhile, broke camp and began moving toward the Little Bighorn River (Robinson, 2001, 182–84).

Meanwhile, on the Yellowstone, Terry's forces had finally linked with Gibbon's. On June 16, a scouting detail of six companies of Seventh Cavalry under Major Marcus A. Reno

The Seventh departed about noon June 22, moving down along the Rosebud. Over the next two days, the column found signs of the great Native American camp. At dusk on June 24, Lieutenant Charles Varnum took some of the Crow Native American scouts to a height overlooking the Little Bighorn Valley, and saw the camp some 18 miles (30 km) away along the Little Bighorn. Custer got his men moving again. He hoped to conceal them in the hills dividing the Rosebud and Little Bighorn valleys, rest them, scout the Native American camp, and then attack at dawn, June 26.

At daylight, Sunday, June 25, he ordered a halt for coffee, while he joined Varnum and the scouts on the height. As they pointed out the camp, they also noticed Native Americans from the village watching them. Custer decided to attack immediately. Moving his troops into the Little Bighorn Valley, he divided them into three battalions, sending one under Captain Frederick W. Benteen up the valley to cut off retreat, and one, under Reno, across the river to attack the village from the front. He would follow the ridges and hit from the rear.

After a forced march over rough terrain, Reno charged the village shortly before 3:00 PM. Before reaching it, however, his exhausted, thirsty horses became unmanageable, forcing him to dismount and form a line. Taken by surprise, the Native Americans quickly recovered and organized a counterattack, and Reno was forced back into some timber near the river. As the hostiles began moving in among the trees, he realized he was vulnerable, and organized a retreat across the river and up into the ridges. The retreat fell apart at the riverbank. Hostile Native Americans moved in among the soldiers, cutting them into small groups, knocking them from their horses and killing them. Reno managed to reach the top of a ridge with the remnants of his battered

found one of the campsites of the giant village, and soon located the trail. The next day, they followed the trail up the Rosebud, unaware of the battle Crook was then fighting 60 miles (100 km) upriver. Finally, Reno turned back toward the Yellowstone, reporting the information to Terry on June 20. Terry decided to send Custer with the cavalry to circle around and press the Native Americans from the south, while Gibbon's infantry pressured them from the north. Thus if one column actually became embroiled in a fight, the other would be close enough to assist—assuming, of course, that Custer would allow the infantry time to get into position. If the Native Americans decided not to fight, the two converging columns would block a successful retreat and bring them under control (Terry, 4).

Only six months after the Custer disaster at Little Bighorn, Frederick Whittaker published a highly romanticized biography of his former Union Army commander that served as the basis for much of the Custer mystique. This illustration from the book was one of the first to depict the so-called "Last Stand," but like so many of the era, is totally imaginary. (Author's collection)

command, where he found a natural depression to serve as a makeshift fort.

Benteen, meanwhile, determined that he was on a fool's errand. Receiving a message from Custer to return to the main column with the ammunition packs, he turned about and

building a defense (Overfield, 40–41).

Custer was unaware of what had befallen Reno. The last thing he had seen was Reno charging across the plain toward the village. A short time later he sent a courier to Benteen with a message to join him with the ammunition packs. Then, after a probe at the center of the village, he returned to the ridges, leaving three companies under Captain Myles Keogh overlooking the village near that point, while Captain George W. Yates took two companies to the far end. Custer set up headquarters on a rise between the two groups.

The first attack came against Keogh's line, which appears to have collapsed. Yates placed one of his companies in line, and detached the other to support Keogh. Then his line collapsed, and the Native Americans moved in among the troopers with knives, hatchets, and clubs. The survivors gathered on the rise around Custer, where the officers seemed to have restored some sort of order. By then, however, it was too late. The five companies were annihilated.

Several miles upriver, Reno's men dug in. Sniping continued until nightfall, and throughout the next day. Late Monday, the Native Americans finally broke camp, separated into individual bands, and began moving out of the valley. On Tuesday, June 27, Gibbon's column, accompanied by General Terry, found the bodies of Custer's troops, and rescued Reno's beleaguered command. (The disaster at the Little Bighorn is one of the most heavily discussed subjects. Among the many recent works are Fox; Gray; Robinson, 1995; Sklenar; and Utley, 1988).

News of the disaster arrived in the East amid the celebration of the nation's centennial. It cast a pall of gloom over the celebration, created a furor, and the public demanded vengeance. On Sheridan's orders, Miles and Mackenzie were transferred north with their regiments. The government authorized the construction of two new military posts, and the army was expanded. Sherman instructed Sheridan to remove the agents of Red Cloud and Spotted Tail, and replace them with local military commanders.

arrived at the river just as Reno's men were fleeing up on the ridge. Believing that his own inexperienced troops would have no chance against so many warriors, he consolidated with Reno rather than continuing on to Custer. Together the two officers began

The powerful Brulé Lakota chief Spotted Tail grudgingly supported the government during the Great Sioux War of 1876–77. Appointed head chief of all the Sioux, he held that position until his assassination during a tribal political dispute in 1881. (Smithsonian Institute)

Food and equipment could only be issued to Native Americans actually present for roll call, and any that were either absent or subsequently left would be treated as enemies. "We must not have another massacre like Custer[']s," Sherman said, "and Congress is now in session willing to give us all we want" (United States Department of War, record group 393, Special File, Sioux War).

There was one bit of good news. The Fifth Cavalry under its new commander, Colonel Wesley Merritt, was marching to join Crook when it encountered a large hostile band at Warbonnet Creek, Nebraska, on July 16. The Native Americans were beaten and scattered. Although the fight was little more than a skirmish, it was the first real victory of the war and, coming on the heels of the Custer debacle, gave public morale a much-needed

boost (Robinson, 1995, Chapter 22).

After spending much of the summer since the Rosebud fight hunting and fishing at Goose Creek, Crook finally broke camp on August 5, and headed north with almost 2,000 men. To move rapidly, they left their wagons, bedding, baggage, and all but the most basic food and equipment. Despite the time of year, an early winter was setting in. The temperature dropped alarmingly, and rain was almost continuous. The troops were cold, wet, and hungry. Five days later, they linked with Terry, and the two columns followed the Native American trail from the Rosebud over to the Tongue River. As time passed, it grew increasingly obvious that almost 5,000 men commanded by two brigadier-generals would never catch roaming bands of Native Americans. Crook's horses were giving out, and many of the cavalry had to lead them on foot through the mud. Although Terry's men were well provisioned, Crook's rations were reduced to sugar, bacon, and hardtack, and men had only enough coffee to brew one cup at a time (King, August 18, 1876; Finerty, 255–56; Robinson, 1995, 237–38).

On August 24, the command reached the Yellowstone, where Crook replenished from steamboats that supplied Terry. Then he struck out on his own, on an ordeal known to history as the Horse Meat or Starvation March. By the time he had reached the Heart River, 200 miles (320 km) north of the Black Hills, he could feed his troops only two more days on half-rations. Nevertheless, he opted to march to the Black Hills, where he believed the settlements were threatened with attack.

The rain continued. Mud balled up around the hooves of the horses and mules, damaging their feet. Every time an infantryman took a step, several pounds of muck stuck to his shoes. One of Crook's aides, Lieutenant Walter S. Schuyler, wrote to his father, "I have seen men become so exhausted that they were actually insane, but there was no way of carrying them, except for some mounted officer or man to give them his own horse ... I saw men who were very plucky, sit down and cry like children

This drawing of Crook's fight at the Rosebud is romanticized, but nevertheless shows the desperate nature of the struggle, which nearly resulted in Crook's annihilation. These same Native Americans destroyed Custer only eight days later. (Author's collection)

because they could not hold out." As for meals, he said, "water and tightened belts" (Schuyler, November 1, 1876, 87).

Worn-out horses and mules were shot and butchered for food. On September 7, Crook ordered Captain Anson Mills to take 150 men and escort the Commissary Department to the Black Hills settlements. Mills departed that evening. As Crook resumed the march the next morning, a courier arrived with the message that Mills had engaged a large village at Slim Buttes. When he arrived, he found Mills' troops had taken the village and driven the Native Americans down into a ravine, where many more were killed. The men resupplied from Native American provisions, which would ration them for another two days, and destroyed the village. On September 13, the exhausted, hungry command collapsed near Bear Butte, not far from Deadwood, and soon, wagons loaded with food were rumbling in (Robinson, 2001, 192–97).

Although Crook's men were suffering, the Native Americans were even worse off. The constant pressure from the soldiers forced them to keep moving, and stay close to their camps. They were unable to hunt and lay in supplies of food for winter, and their own ponies began to starve. Many realized their situation was hopeless, and started back toward the reservations (Neihardt, 134).

At the agencies, meanwhile, the Native Americans were placed under military rule. On August 15, congress approved an ultimatum that forced them to surrender the unceded lands of Montana and Wyoming, as well as the entire Great Sioux Reservation west of the 103rd meridian, which included the Black Hills. They would receive no further rations until they agreed. They were also expected to draw rations on the Missouri River, where they would be controlled, and to become self-supporting by white standards. In other words, they would surrender or starve (Gray, 260–62).

Although Red Cloud did not openly join the hostiles, he was sympathetic. He and another chief, Red Leaf, took their bands and moved to Chadron Creek, about 20 miles (32 km) northeast of Camp Robinson.

LEFT (BOTH) Crook's Horsemeat March. (US Military Academy Library, West Point, New York)

Determined to make an example of Red Cloud, Mackenzie's men surrounded their camps, and marched them to Camp Robinson, where they were disarmed and unhorsed. Then Crook formally deposed Red Cloud as head chief of the Lakotas, and appointed Spotted Tail in his place (Robinson, 1995, 264–67).

Crook organized yet another expedition, with the cavalry arm commanded by Mackenzie, and the infantry by Lieutenant Colonel Richard Irving Dodge. On November 25, 1876, five months to the day after the Little Bighorn, Mackenzie's troops attacked a major Cheyenne village on the Red Fork of the Powder river. After hard fighting, the Native Americans retreated into the surrounding hills, leaving the soldiers in possession of the camp, where many souvenirs of the Little Bighorn were found. The lodges and winter stores were destroyed, leaving the Cheyennes completely destitute and effectively knocking them out of the war (Robinson, 1995, 296–301).

In Terry's department, meanwhile, conduct of the war now was left exclusively to Miles. Despite the problems other officers experienced during the previous winter, he was determined that "if the Native Americans could live in that country in skin tents in winter ... we, with all our better appliances could be so equipped not only to exist in tents, but also to move under all circumstances." Accordingly, he planned carefully, and requisitioned adequate equipment to chase the Native Americans down regardless of season or

Crook's horsemeat march. (US Military Academy Library, West Point, New York)

weather (Miles, 1:218–19).

Miles' main opponent was Sitting Bull, whose disillusioned chiefs were growing tired of the war. After an abortive attack on a government wagon train, Sitting Bull met with Miles on October 21. Nothing was settled, but Miles' knowledge of Sitting Bull's plans, obtained through Native American spies, unnerved the chief. The two met again the following day, and Miles gave Sitting Bull an ultimatum: he could return to his camp unmolested, but if he had not submitted to the government in 15 minutes, the troops would open fire. As the Native Americans withdrew, they set fire to the grass to cover their movements. Miles sent scouts to stop them, and fighting began. After outflanking the Native Americans, the infantry formed into classic squares, forcing the Native Americans out on a plain where artillery opened up. Finally the Native Americans retreated and the soldiers went into camp, although sniping continued back and forth all night (Miles, 1:121ff.; Greene, 83ff.).

For many of the chiefs in Sitting Bull's camp, this was enough. They broke away, and began heading to the agencies and military posts to surrender. Sitting Bull and about 400 followers started north, eventually seeking refuge in Canada.

With Sitting Bull neutralized, Miles turned his attention to Crazy Horse. On January 7–8, 1877, his soldiers attacked Crazy Horse's camp at Wolf Mountain in southern Montana. The second day of the fight, the Native Americans took refuge among the bluffs, forcing the infantry to charge. Hand-to-hand fighting ensued, just as a blizzard blew in which, according to Miles, "added an inexpressible weirdness to the scene." With resistance effectively smashed, he started his troops back north, to get them into the shelter of their post (Miles, 1:238).

Throughout the spring, Native Americans sought out the officers they felt would give them the best terms for surrender. Miles, a self-made soldier who disdained the military obsession with regulation and policy, was determined to be magnanimous and immediately enlisted surrendered warriors as army scouts, before the government could otherwise dispose of them. Although Crook

Miles (4) stands with members of his staff as he prepares for a march that resulted in the defeat of Crazy Horse in January 1877. Miles sports a beard against winter cold, and wears his distinctive bearskin coat. The Native Americans called him "Bearcoat" and referred to his hard-driving Fifth Infantry as the "Walk-a-Heaps." (Little Bighorn Battlefield National Monument)

Miles' infantrymen level their long Springfield rifles during a raging snowstorm at the battle of Wolf Mountain, in January 1877, in this drawing by Frederick Remington. (Author's collection)

sympathized with the Native Americans, he was a West Pointer and a career soldier who ultimately obeyed the government mandate of removal. Those who surrendered to him often found themselves transported to the Native American Territory for internment on the reservations there (Robinson, 2001, 214, 226).

On May 7, 1877, Miles' troops captured a large camp of Miniconjous under the chief Lame Deer, who was killed in the fight. This action essentially ended the Great Sioux War although, as with the Red River War, mop-up operations would continue for another year or so. Now, with the great tribes of both the Northern and Southern Plains broken, the complete government control of the central two-thirds of the United States was assured. Part of that control was the policy of removal and concentration of the tribes to the Native American Territory.

Survivors

The battle of the Little Bighorn was a pivotal event. For the Native Americans, it was perhaps their greatest single victory, one in which they completely annihilated five companies of a modern army. Yet it was a hollow victory because it outraged the nation, and assured the ultimate destruction of the Native American way of life. As such, the Little Bighorn left an indelible imprint on those who fought there. Well into the 20th century, both Native American and white survivors had vivid recollections of that day. Among them were the Cheyenne warrior Wooden Leg (1858–1940), and Sergeant Charles Windolph (1851–1950), Company H, Seventh Cavalry, who is believed to have been the last white survivor.

Wooden Leg

Wooden Leg began relating his story to Dr. Thomas Marquis, former physician to the Northern Cheyenne Agency in Montana, in the 1920s. Although Marquis did not speak Cheyenne, he was reasonably fluent in Plains sign. This was the primary means of communication, although Wooden Leg sometimes would emphasize a point with words from his limited English vocabulary, and augment his gestures with pencil sketches. Other Cheyennes who were either present at the fight, or among the bands hostile to the government in 1876, often participated in the discussions, corroborated Wooden Leg's experiences, and offered their own views on the subject (Marquis, n.d., vii–ix).

Wooden Leg was born on the Cheyenne river in the Black Hills of South Dakota in 1858. His name referred to physical stamina—the ability to walk long distances without tiring as though his legs were made of wood. He earned it when he and some

companions lost their mounts to Crow horse thieves. On foot, they overtook two of the Crows, rushed and killed them, and recovered their horses (Marquis, n.d., 1–5).

Growing up, Wooden Leg was typical of a Cheyenne boy training to be a warrior and provider. He learned to ride and hunt, and through painful experience of snowblindness and frostbite, how to handle himself outdoors. The only hostile encounter with whites came when he was about seven or eight years old, when members of his band fought soldiers— probably Connor's—on Lodgepole Creek near its confluence with the North Platte. His own first combat experiences were against Crows and Shoshones, the traditional enemies of the Cheyennes. When Wooden Leg was about eight, his older brother, Strong Wind Blowing, and another Cheyenne were killed in the Fetterman massacre.

"There was rejoicing in our camp on account of the victory," he said, "But our family and all relatives of the two dead Cheyennes were in mourning. We wept and prayed for the spirits of our lost ones" (Marquis, n.d., 14–15).

Wooden Leg was in Two Moon's camp when Reynolds attacked it on March 17, 1876. He had no ammunition for his old muzzle-loading rifle, and had loaned his revolver to his cousin, who had gone out with the scouts the night before. He did have a borrowed bow and arrows, and grabbed the first pony he saw, to go out and fight. It soon became obvious that the camp was lost, so he returned to his lodge to gather his valuables. As he rode out, he picked up two children, carried them to safety, and then went back into the fray. When he and three companions killed and stripped a soldier, he came away with the man's blue coat. From a distance, they watched as the soldiers burned their village. Later, they recovered what they could

Wooden Leg, a Cheyenne warrior shown here in 1927, participated in virtually every major battle of the Great Sioux War, including the Rosebud and the Little Bighorn. (Little Bighorn Battlefield National Monument)

from the wreckage, and that night, Wooden Leg was among the group that stampeded the horses (Marquis, n.d., 165–69).

The Cheyennes joined Crazy Horse's Oglalas, and together the two groups traveled up and joined the giant camp of the Hunkpapas under Sitting Bull. Wooden Leg participated in the battle of the Rosebud, after which the camp moved toward the Little Bighorn. The Cheyenne camp circle was at the north end, downriver from Reno's attack, and so these warriors were primarily concerned with Custer. Describing the fight, Wooden Leg recalled (Marquis, n.d., 230, 234):

Most of the Native Americans were working around the ridge … occupied by the soldiers. We were lying down in gullies and behind sagebrush hillocks. The shooting at first was at a distance,

but we kept creeping in closer around the ridge. Bows and arrows were in use much more than guns. From the hiding-places of the Indians, the arrows could be shot in a high and long curve, to fall upon the soldiers or their horses. An Indian using a gun had to jump up and expose himself long enough to shoot …

I saw one Sioux walking slowly toward the gulch, going away from where were the soldiers. He wabbled [sic] dizzily as he moved along. He fell down, got up, fell down again, got up again. As he passed near to where I was I saw that his whole lower jaw was shot away. The sight of him made me sick. I had to vomit.

After the battle, the tribes split up. In November, while the main Cheyenne band camped on the Red Fork of the Powder River, Wooden Leg and nine other warriors went out searching for Crow Native Americans. They passed through the Little Bighorn, and collected unfired cartridges and souvenirs scattered about the battlefield. As they headed back toward their camp, they encountered their people who, during their absence, had been attacked by Mackenzie.

"They had but little food," Wooden Leg said. "Many of them had no blankets nor robes. They had no lodges. Only here and there was there one wearing moccasins. The others had their feet wrapped in loose pieces of skin or of cloth. Women, children and old people were straggling along over the snow-covered trail down the valley" (Marquis, n.d., 282–86).

Following the surrender, Wooden Leg was among the group exiled to the Native American Territory. He did not, however, join Dull Knife or Little Wolf in the outbreak, but waited until he and other Northern Cheyennes were allowed to repatriate. He later became a baptized Christian and a judge of the Indian Court (Thrapp, 3:1594).

Sergeant Charles Windolph

Wooden Leg's army counterpart, Sergeant Charles Windolph, was with Captain Frederick Benteen's battalion at the Little

Infantrymen and Native American scouts mop up Dull Knife's camp on the Powder River on November 25, 1876, after Mackenzie's cavalry captured it. The fight destroyed Cheyenne military power forever. This drawing is by famous Western artist Frederick Remington. (Author's collection)

Bighorn. He was in his 80s and living in Lead, South Dakota, when historian Frazier Hunt first contacted him in the mid-1930s. Over the next 10 years, until 1946, he related his story to Hunt and his son, Robert. The following year, it was published "with explanatory material and contemporary sidelights on the Custer Fight," as *I Fought With Custer*. Although Windolph commented that the 70 years since the fight had given him plenty of time to remember the details and fix them in his mind, he acknowledged his account might not match those of other survivors. "Even the men who were with Benteen and Reno and lived to tell the tale, didn't come anywhere near telling the same stories about what they did, and what they saw," he explained, adding, "I had only one pair of eyes, so, of course, all I can tell is what I saw myself" (Hunt and Hunt, 1–2).

Windolph was born in Bergen, Prussia, on December 9, 1851. He reached military age as Prussia was preparing to go to war with France, and to avoid the draft, he escaped first to Sweden, and later to the United States. Like many other young German draft dodgers, he found it difficult to earn a living in the United States, and so ended up with the only job available—enlistment in the US Army (Hunt and Hunt, 3–4).

Company H, Seventh Cavalry, was posted to Nashville, Tennessee, when Windolph joined in 1870. Three years later, his battalion was sent to Dakota Territory (North Dakota), where he took part in the Yellowstone Expedition, to explore a route for the railroad into Montana. He was not present in the expedition's only Native American fight on August 4, because Company H had been left behind to guard the supply depot on the lower Yellowstone. The following year, he participated in Custer's Black Hills Expedition. After a brief stint in New Orleans during the winter of 1875–76, his company was sent to Fort Abraham Lincoln.

On May 17, the Seventh rode out of Fort Abraham Lincoln as part of General Terry's

Dakota Column. Windolph remembered the day (Hunt and Hunt, 53):

You felt like you were somebody when you were on a good horse, with a carbine dangling from its small leather ring socket on your McClelland [sic] saddle, and a Colt army revolver strapped on your hip; and a hundred rounds of ammunition in your web belt and in your saddle pockets. You were a cavalryman of the Seventh Regiment. You were a part of a proud outfit that had a fighting reputation, and you were ready for a fight or a frolic (Hunt, 53).

The Dakota Column linked up with Gibbon's Montana Column, and on June 22, the Seventh separated and started on its scouting expedition. Windolph recalled that although the men expected a hard fight, they were not particularly worried. Each man believed that if anyone died, it would be someone else, not himself. On June 25, after a hard three days, Seventh located the Native American village and prepared to attack.

About noon, Benteen took his battalion, including Company H, up the valley and scouted the hills, while Custer and Reno moved down the valley toward the village. After about two hours, Benteen ordered the battalion to turn about and rejoin the others. As they drew closer, they heard gunfire, Benteen ordered his men to draw pistols, and they charged up the bluffs at a gallop to find Reno and his men fleeing up the hill.

"I'll never forget that first glimpse I had of the hilltop," Windolph said. "Here were a little group of men in blue, forming a skirmish line, while their beaten comrades, disorganized and terror stricken, were making their way on foot and on horseback up the narrow coulee that led from the river, 150 feet (30 m) below" (Hunt and Hunt, 96).

For the next several hours until sundown, the two battalions held off the Native Americans, all the while wondering why Custer didn't come to support them. It never occurred to them that Custer and the remaining five companies of the Seventh were already dead. After a cold, rainy night, the shooting began again. By now the wounded were crying for water, and Benteen called for volunteers to make the near suicidal rush to the river. Windolph was one of 17 who came forward, and Benteen detailed him and three other good marksmen to draw fire and keep the Native Americans distracted while the others went for water. Several of the water party were wounded, but Windolph and his three German countrymen emerged unscathed. All four received the Medal of Honor (Hunt and Hunt, 104–05).

After the Native Americans withdrew, and Terry and Gibbon arrived, the men learned of Custer's fate. Windolph was a member of the detail that buried Custer and his brother, Tom.

After the Great Sioux War, Windolph participated in the Nez Percé campaign of 1877. He left the army in 1883, and worked for Homestake Mining Company in Lead, for 49 years. He died on March 11, 1950, at the age of 98 (Thrapp, 3:1582).

The slow move toward Native American rights

During the period immediately following the Civil War, the majority of the American people, which is to say those living east of the Mississippi, were relatively indifferent to the conditions on the plains. The Native American situation was a mere abstraction. The four exhausting years of internal conflict, the horrendous drain of blood and treasure, and the devastation in the South and the border states, were a reality. The reaction to the Red Cloud War demonstrated the public's lack of enthusiasm for a Native American campaign. Native American fighting would be bloody and expensive (the Great Sioux War alone ultimately cost $2,312,531.24, a staggering figure for the time). The government was pressured to develop the nation, and do whatever was necessary to encourage that development while avoiding conflict. Indeed, one of the reasons a commission was appointed to negotiate the Medicine Lodge and Fort Laramie Treaties was to convince the Native Americans to allow development to proceed unmolested.

When conflicts did occur, life in the East went on, often oblivious to the fact that a war was even under way. In 1876, the year the Great Sioux War began, Alexander Graham Bell invented the telephone, Samuel L. Clemens, better known as Mark Twain, published *The Adventures of Tom Sawyer*, and professional baseball teams organized the National League. Colorado became a state, joining the existing plains states of Kansas, Nebraska, Nevada, and Texas. John D. Rockefeller was busy consolidating the oil industry, and the dominant economic force was steel (Robinson, *Good Year to Die*, xxi–xxii).

Canada was settling its great plains simultaneously with the United States, but the history of the two movements could not have been more opposite. When the North West Mounted Police was organized in 1873, many predicted it would have the same bitter experience as the US Army south of the border. The 300,000 square miles (776,996 km²) under its jurisdiction had problems identical to those of the United States, i.e. tens of thousands of disenchanted Native Americans, whiskey peddlers who profited from Native American discontent, and a large helping of American badmen who had fled across the border to escape prosecution in their own country. Many of the Native American tribes were related to, or allied with, the American Lakotas, who themselves frequently fled north across the "medicine line" to take refuge in British territory. However, the Mountie had an advantage over his American counterpart in a rigorous training program that prepared and conditioned him for his assignment. Other factors were stringent discipline and careful attention to equipment necessary for the job ahead.

The first encounter between Mounties and Plains Native Americans came on August 13, 1874, when a detachment en route to Fort Edmonton, Alberta, encountered about 30 dirty, hungry Sioux. The men's reaction was more of curiosity than hostility, and soon the Mounties and Native Americans were sitting together, smoking and exchanging pleasantries through their Native American and Métis (mixed-blood) scouts. The Native Americans were told that Queen Victoria was the mother of all Canadians, regardless of race, that she loved all her children equally, and would not allow any of her children to take unfair advantage of the others. This meeting set the pattern for their future relations with any Native Americans. Thus, the Canadian Plains were settled without a shot ever being exchanged between Mountie and Native American (Tanner, Chapter 5).

If Canada resolved its Native American question peacefully, Mexico was an entirely different matter. As noted earlier, the US conflict with the Southern Plains Native Americans was inherited from Spain and Mexico. The Kiowas especially were notorious for raiding into that country, and Mexican captives were even adopted into the tribe. One reason for the failure of the Fort Atkinson Treaty was the US insistence that raids into Mexico cease, and that all Mexican captives be repatriated (Mooney, 173).

During the first four decades of its independence, Mexico failed to achieve political stability. The country was divided between a conservative faction centered in Mexico City and consisting of the large landholders, clergy, and army, and the liberals who dominated the provinces. Although the country's first president, Major General Guadalupe Victoria, managed to finish his term, few, if any of his successors did. In 1858, the country was plunged into a vicious three-year civil war between the Mexico City conservatives and the liberal reformers. No sooner was that resolved and the reformers gained power than Mexico was invaded by the French, who, in concert with the conservatives, installed the Austrian Archduke Maximilian on the throne. With the ousting of the French and the execution of Maximilian, the country was devastated and needed complete internal reorganization. Mexico was unable to defend its own frontier from Native American raids from the United States, nor was it capable of preventing Native Americans from Mexico from raiding into the US (Parkes).

The border between the US and Mexico was not a "medicine line," as was the border with Canada. US troops had little compunction about chasing Native Americans well into Mexico. And because the Native Americans routinely raided there, they were in enemy territory regardless of which side of the border they were on, and behaved accordingly. The establishment of the authoritarian regime of Porfirio Diaz at the end of 1876 inaugurated more than three decades of relative stability, and Mexican

troops began actively suppressing Native American outbreaks. As time passed, the US and Mexican governments reached an accommodation whereby the military of either country could cross into the other in "hot pursuit" of raiding Native American bands. From the US viewpoint, the term "hot pursuit" became so broadly defined that American troops sometimes employed scouts to lead them to major Native American camps deep in the mountains of Mexico.

One reason for public ignorance of events on the plains was lack of reliable and reasonably current information. Not until the late 1860s was there serious newspaper coverage of Native American fighting. Instead, eastern editorial staffers who never left their offices wrote largely imaginary accounts. This began to change in 1867, when Joseph Wasson, co-owner of the Silver City, Idaho, *Owyhee Avalanche*, accompanied then-Lieutenant Colonel George Crook on an expedition against the Native Americans of the Pacific northwest. Wasson's dispatches were reprinted in the *San Francisco Evening Bulletin*, giving metropolitan readers their first eyewitness reports of a Native American campaign. Aware that a well-cultivated public image might lead to advancement (it did), Crook continued to encourage correspondents, not only in the northwest, but also during his campaigns in Arizona and on the plains. Soon, professional correspondents from New York, Chicago, Denver, and elsewhere accompanied expeditions against Native Americans, and soldiers augmented their meager army pay by selling their accounts to the newspapers. Correspondents Wasson and Robert Strahorn took an active part in the fighting during Crook's campaigns, and Mark Kellogg died with Custer at the Little Bighorn (Knight, 31–32; 2001, 94, 164–65).

The Native American Wars reached their climax during the decade of the 1870s, but during much of that time, the eastern part of the nation was preoccupied with the economic depression, known to history as the Panic of 1873. The crisis began on September 18, 1873, when the New York banking firm

Brigadier General George Crook (seated second from right) poses with staff, scouts, and friends outside Fort Fetterman, Wyoming, during a lull in the fighting in 1876. Crook, who eschewed military formality, preferred a civilian suit and white sun helmet in the field, and rarely wore a uniform even at his headquarters. (US Army Military History Institute)

of Jay Cooke & Co. went bankrupt. Cooke's interests were extensive, including control of the Northern Pacific Railroad, then under construction across the Northern Plains. Two days later, the New York Stock Exchange was forced to suspend trading. Over the next six years, more than a million people— one-fortieth of the entire population—lost their jobs. For those still employed, wages fell 20 percent although there was no significant reduction in the cost of living (McFeely, 392–93). Many took to the roads, and when word reached the East about the discovery of gold in the Black Hills, they headed for the Dakotas in hopes of a fresh start.

Arriving in Wyoming at the height of the rush, in February 1876, Bourke wrote (Diary, 3:2–3):

In Cheyenne, we could see and hear nothing but "Black Hills." Every store advertises its inducements as an outfitting agency, every wagon is chartered to convea [sic] freight to the new Pactolus. The Q[uarter]. M[aster]. Dept. experiences grave difficulty in finding the transportation needed by the Army at the different camps. Everything is bound for the Black Hills. Cheyenne is full of people and her merchants and saloon keepers are doing a rushing business. Great numbers of new buildings, mostly brick, have been erected during the past six months, giving the town a bustle and activity as well as an appearance of advancement in favorable contrast with Omaha, Denver and Salt Lake … I saw many adventurers journeying to the Black Hills; their wagons and animals looked new and good as a general thing and the supplies carried ample in quantity. However, there were many on foot and without adequate sustenance and some begging their way from ranch to ranch along the trail … It is strongly suggestive of the want and misery of the Eastern states that so many people should rush upon slight stimulus towards the new El Dorado.

Gold and goldrushes were among the most obvious signs of advancing technology that was pushing the Native Americans aside. Prior to the Civil War, however, the great concern of Eastern reformers was the abolition of slavery. Once that was accomplished, they turned their attention westward, and President Grant's Board of Native American Commissioners and his Peace Policy were among the results. However, there was no serious, coordinated plan or effort. The movement gained impetus in 1879, when a group of Ponca Native Americans took their grievances to court. The problem had its origins nine years earlier when in the Fort Laramie Treaty, by bureaucratic error, Ponca lands on the Missouri River were ceded to the Lakotas as part of the Great Sioux Reservation. When the government decided to relocate the Lakota Agencies to the Missouri River in 1876, it was deemed expedient to remove the Poncas to the Native American Territory. Interior Secretary Carl Schurz rationalized that, because the Lakotas and Poncas were ancient enemies, this would be in the best interests of the latter tribe.

Relocation began during the spring of 1877, and many Poncas died en route. Many more died in the hot, malarial climate of Oklahoma. In early spring 1879, the only son of the Ponca chief Standing Bear died of malaria. Standing Bear, who had already lost two daughters in the relocation, decided to bury the boy in his old country. Thirty others joined him on the march from Oklahoma, across Kansas and Nebraska, walking along behind a wagon carrying the boy's coffin. On reaching their home country, the Omahas welcomed them on their reservation, allowing them to settle and plant crops. The government, however, was unwilling to tolerate this breach of established policy, and ordered General Crook to arrest the Poncas and send them back to the territory (Howard, 32–36).

Crook was less than enthusiastic. With his connivance, and perhaps even at his suggestion, the Poncas' story was sent to metropolitan newspapers from Chicago to New York. Citizens' committees formed in Omaha, where the Poncas were interned, and in Yankton, capital of Dakota Territory (South Dakota). The case demonstrated that the government's solution—relocation from ancient lands and concentration in the Native American Territory—was a failure, and galvanized the Eastern humanitarians into action (Mardock, 173).

The guiding forces were General Crook and Thomas Henry Tibbles, former abolitionist and preacher who now was assistant editor of the *Omaha Daily Herald*. Tibbles believed the case hinged on whether the equal protection guarantees under the Fourteenth Amendment to the Constitution applied to Native Americans. At his behest, two of the Midwest's leading attorneys took the case *pro bono* and filed a writ of *habeas corpus*.

United States ex. rel. Ma-chu-nah-zah (Standing Bear) vs. George Crook was heard before US District Judge Elmer Dundy in Omaha on April 30, 1879. Crook was named as defendant in his capacity as the officer responsible for enforcing the government edict, but made no secret of his sympathies with the Poncas. The government's response was that a Native American was a ward of the government, and therefore had no legal standing in court (Tibbles, 1973, 199–200, and 1995, 34ff.).

After all the arguments were heard, Standing Bear addressed the court. His simple statement, that he was a human being with the same feelings, hopes, and dreams of any human being, reduced Judge Dundy to tears. A week later, he issued his ruling—just as Native Americans were expected to obey the laws of the United States, so were they entitled to the protection of those laws. The detention of the Poncas, he declared, was in violation of that protection, and they were ordered released (Tibbles, 1995, 108–11; Robinson, 2001, 238–39).

Riding the momentum, Tibbles arranged for Standing Bear to make a speaking tour of the eastern states, attracting more people to the Native American cause. The activists found an ally in Crook. Like many soldiers, he had initially viewed them as naive busybodies who knew nothing of the situation, and had advocated a military solution. Yet, from the beginning of his career as a young lieutenant on the West Coast, he had always believed that the settlers and government had provoked much of the trouble that required military action. Even before the Ponca case, he had commented to Tibbles, "The buffalo is gone, and a Indian can't catch enough jack rabbits to subsist himself and family, and then there aren't enough jack rabbits to catch. What are they to do? Starvation is staring them in the face ... I do not wonder, and you will not either, that when these Indians see their wives and children starving, and their last sources of supplies cut off, they go to war. And then we are sent out there to kill them. It is an outrage" (*Army and Navy Journal*, 29 July 1878). The Standing Bear case, where Native Americans had used the legal system to achieve their goals, convinced him that there were alternatives.

Unfortunately the Native American rights activists never could agree on an agenda. An extreme faction believed the Native Americans should be given immediate citizenship under the Fourteenth Amendment, after which the need for assimilation into 19th-century society could be considered. Moderates agreed with Secretary Schurz that there would have to be a long period of government stewardship to ease the Native Americans away from tribal life in slow stages. Ultimately, the basic question of a future for the Native Americans became lost in rhetoric and ideology (Robinson, 2001, 239–40).

The Ponca chief Standing Bear initiated a legal case that was one of the first steps in establishing the rights of Native Americans as residents of the United States. (Nebraska State Historical Society)

Women and children

The brutal realities

There was nothing romantic or noble about Plains Native American life. It was a life of hardship, and a struggle for survival from dawn to dark, with each person doing his or her assigned task.

The role of the women was only dimly understood by whites, who often used the standards of their own civilization as a measure of Native American life. An officer posted to Fort Sill, Native American Territory, in the 1870s wrote that Kiowa women were little more than "slaves" (Myers, Folder 10). In fact, the relationship was not bondage so much as a division of labor. The warrior fought the wars, conducted the raids, made and repaired weapons, undertook the often grueling and dangerous task of hunting for food, and raised ponies, the commodity by which Plains Native Americans reckoned wealth. The women gathered plant foods, cooked the meals, prepared the hides of animals killed by their male relatives, made and repaired the clothing and tipis, tended the children, and whatever other tasks were to be done around camp.

Although the Native American women rarely were combatants, they often accompanied their men into battle or on raids. During the Warren Wagon Train Massacre in Texas in 1871, two Kiowa women stood off to one side, encouraging the warriors with shrill tongue-rattling (Nye, 129). At the battle of the Little Bighorn in 1876, a Cheyenne woman known as Kate Bighead remained on the fringes, singing war songs to encourage her nephew who was in the fight (Marquis, 1987, 89).

With some exceptions, such as the Minnesota uprising, Native American prisoners usually received consideration from regular soldiers, who viewed Native American fighting simply as a duty. Military prisoners were interned at a fort, then placed on a reservation, and those considered most incorrigible might be sent to Fort Marion. Those who fell into the hands of citizens or local volunteer troops, however, were not always so fortunate. The ongoing raids back and forth kindled deep hatreds among the settlers, who were not always concerned about distinguishing between friendly and hostile bands. The vicious mutilation of the Native American bodies following the Sand Creek Massacre demonstrated what whites were capable of.

Nelson Lee

Among white settlers and travelers, one of the greatest fears was being taken alive. With few exceptions, captivity for adult males meant a slow, hideous death, while women and even young girls might be brutalized. One of the few adult males to survive was Nelson Lee, a former Texas Ranger, who spent three years as a captive. In the spring of 1855, Lee joined a company formed by William Aikens, to drive mules from Texas to the California market. Shortly after midnight on April 3, Comanches attacked their camp, and all were killed except Lee, Aikens, Thomas Martin, and John Stewart. The Native Americans tied up Lee and Aikens facing each other, and made them watch while Stewart and Martin were scalped alive, tortured, and murdered. Then for whatever reason Lee and Aikens were allowed to dress and return to their tents. Aikens later was sent away with another band, while Lee continued on with his captors to their main camp. Here, he forestalled any thoughts of killing him by making himself useful, to the point they nicknamed him *Chemakacho* meaning Good White Man (Lee, 104–08, 115).

Several months later, three white women were brought into camp. They identified themselves as Mrs. Henrietta Haskins, and her daughters, Margaret, and Harriet. They were survivors from a party of English Mormon emigrants which had been massacred two or three years earlier. The mother, who was feeble and rheumatic, served as "a common drudge," while the daughters were "slaves and wives" of two warriors. During their stay in Lee's camp, Mrs. Haskins' health broke, and she was scalped and slashed to death while her daughters were forced to watch (Lee, 144).

If a female child was captured at an early enough age, she often adapted readily to her situation, grew up as a member of the tribe, and came to identify with the Native Americans and share their animosity toward her own race. Native Americans frequently adopted captive children, both boys and girls, especially on the Southern Plains, where their birthrate was low and the infant mortality rate high. During his captivity, Nelson Lee recalled meeting four white girls, ranging in age from 12 to 18 (Lee, 123):

They knew no other than the language of the Comanches, and in all respects conformed to their manners and customs. It was, therefore, evident to me they had been captured in early childhood and remember no other life than that they were then leading.

Adolescent boys, with their tendency toward rebellion, and desire to assert themselves, often had little trouble adapting to the ways of the Native American warrior. The story of Theodore Adolphus (Dot) Babb, who was captured by Comanches in Texas in September 1865, at the age of 13, is not unusual. With Babb's father and older brother driving cattle to Arkansas, the household consisted of himself, his mother, nine-year-old sister, an infant sister, and a Mrs. Luster, a young Civil War widow who was living with the family. The Native Americans attacked late in the afternoon,

breaking down the door of the house, mortally wounding Mrs. Babb, and carrying off Mrs. Luster and the two older children. That night, Mrs. Luster escaped, although she later was captured by a party of Kiowas. The Comanches, meanwhile, had ascertained that Babb assisted in the escape, and decided to kill him. The boy's defiance, however, won their respect, and they carried him back to their main camp to raise him as a warrior. He adapted readily, participating in raids on other tribes. After two years, he and his sister were ransomed and returned home, although he maintained close ties with his adoptive Comanche family for the rest of his life (Babb, 20–36, 58).

The "glittering misery" of army wives

Although General Sherman believed officers should marry young so their wives might help relieve the isolation of frontier duty, government indifference made life almost unendurable for military dependents. As the wife of one junior officer commented (Boyd, 136):

It is notorious that no provision is made for women in the army. Many indignation meetings were held at which we discussed the matter, and rebelled at being considered mere camp followers. It is a recognized fact that a woman's presence— as a wife—alone prevents demoralization, and army officers are always encouraged to marry.

The most famous army wife of all, Elizabeth Bacon Custer, complained that while the regulations might go into minute detail on such mundane things as how to boil bean soup, wives were totally ignored (Stallard, 16).

The use of the term "camp follower" was no exaggeration. According to army regulations, dependents of soldiers and officers had no legal status other than that of camp followers. Unlike laundresses, who were considered military personnel and entitled to quarters, rations, and the services of the post surgeon, wives were left to their own devices. And where the laundresses had certain specified legal rights, which they invoked with a vengeance, wives were subject to the whims of the post commander, who could even ban them from the post if it suited him. Frequent cuts in military spending led to regulations designed to discourage enlisted men from marrying. Consequently, many enlisted men's wives served as laundresses, and enlisted men sometimes married laundresses. Either arrangement brought the family extra income and rationing (Stallard, 16, 57–59).

The wife of an officer went west for love of her husband, a sense of duty, and a certain amount of romantic idealism about the region. The latter notion was quickly dispelled by reality. At best, their lives involved inconvenience, and at worst, total misery. They left large, comfortable homes in the east, often to live in tents and hovels. Even when reasonably decent housing was available, their positions were not always secure because their husbands could be "ranked out" by senior officers. Frances Boyd, wife of a cavalry lieutenant at Fort Clark, Texas, described the procedure:

I was ill at the time, confined to my room; and messages were brought at intervals from six different officers, who all outranked Mr. Boyd, that each had selected our house. Ridiculous as it may seem, every one was outranked by another. Finally, a captain of the infantry chose our quarters, and then the doctor declared I could not be moved ….

The following day, Mrs. Boyd gave birth to her third child, who immediately contracted whooping cough. Both her other children also came down with it, and she herself was ill from childbed fever. "For a week I was at death's door with fever; and yet the very day baby was four weeks old we were obliged to move, that the captain, who demanded his house without further delay, might be accommodated" (Boyd, 270–72).

For the next two years, the five members of the Boyd family occupied a one-room shanty, while the captain, a bachelor, kept the house. Still, Mrs. Boyd felt better off than another wife who was forced to live in the hallway that separated the duplex quarters of two other officers and their families. One morning her husband was advised that a superior officer wanted the hallway. In disgust, he resigned from the army (Boyd, 273).

When soldiers were in the field in hostile country, wives never knew whether they would see them again. Elizabeth Custer, whose husband died along with half his regiment at the Little Bighorn, wrote of "the terrible parting which seemed a foreshadowing of all the most intense anguish that our Heavenly Father can send to his children" (Custer, 182). As if to aggravate their unhappiness, wives visiting the East during their husbands' campaigns sometimes found that the public was not even aware that a military expedition was under way (Custer, 88).

The uncertainty especially increased if the Native Americans attached to the post began to get uneasy. Many army wives were aware of the incredible efficiency of the so-called "moccasin telegraph," that still-unfathomable means by which Native Americans received news from throughout the plains much more quickly than government couriers could carry it. Although the details might vary as they circulated from one group of Native Americans to the next, the basic information generally was reliable. In early July 1876, at Fort Rice, one of two stations of the Seventh Cavalry, the Native Americans began talking about a massacre involving the entire command. The wives of the officers gathered together in one of the quarters for a sleepless night, waiting for some sort of word. Early the next morning, the Missouri River steamer arrived with mail from the war zone. "Unwashed, uncombed, the thud-thud of our hearts almost suffocating, we dashed to the trader-store post office," the wife of Lieutenant Francis M. Gibson remembered. "All those from forlorn old Fort Rice were safely accounted for—all but one, our dear Jack [Lieutenant Jack Sturgis], so very young, so beloved by us all" (Fougera, 265–66).

Farther north, at Fort Abraham Lincoln, the Seventh's headquarters post, the wives were not so fortunate. Twenty-six women learned that day that they were widows.

Often bodies could not be recovered immediately, and sometimes not at all, denying the widows the comfort of seeing proper funerals and burials. Adding to the emotional pain, the army assumed no responsibility for the widow, who was expected to vacate quarters as soon as possible. The benefits paid to the widow and surviving children were so paltry that Congress considered that it was doing Native American Wars widows a favor in 1908, when it increased their pensions to $12 a month (Stallard, 42).

Martha Summerhayes, herself a soldier's wife, summed up the feelings of all when she wrote, "I fell to thinking: was the army life, then, only glittering misery...?" (Summerhayes, 45).

An unresolved legacy

On November 11, 1865, two Santee chiefs, Medicine Bottle and Shakopee, who had been kidnapped and smuggled out of Canada, were hanged at Fort Snelling, Minnesota, for their part in the 1862 uprising. According to legend, as Shakopee mounted the gallows, he heard the whistle of a railroad locomotive and remarked, "As the white man comes in the Native American goes out" (Carley, 75).

If the story is apocryphal, it was nevertheless prophetic. To some extent, the so-called "Native American Question" went all the way back to Columbus, when the rest of the world learned for the first time that there were other people on the planet besides conventional Europeans, Africans, and Asians. This raised the dilemma of what sort of people they might be, and how to deal with them. The United States inherited the British policy of treating them as sovereign nations. Alone among the people of the United States, Native Americans were specifically exempted by the Constitution from obligations and benefits of citizenship. And while Judge Dundy's ruling in the Standing Bear case essentially gave them protection under the Fourteenth Amendment, it did not establish citizenship, nor could it. Decades earlier, Chief Justice John Marshall had defined the Native American tribes as "domestic dependent nations," with the power to enter into treaties with the federal government. Even that ended in 1871, in part because of the House of Representatives' jealousy of the Senate's treaty-making authority. Henceforth, Native Americans were wards of the government, subject to the joint decisions of both houses of congress. This created yet another bureaucratic stumbling block that was beyond the Native American cultural comprehension (Utley and Washburn, 194; Robinson, 2001, 113).

One of the most devastating government programs was the removal of Native Americans from their home territories, and their concentration in the Native American Territory, without consideration of how the change in environment would affect them. Such was the case with the Northern Cheyennes, who were concentrated with their Southern cousins around Darlington where they could be watched and regulated. The Northern Cheyennes, accustomed to the mountains and valleys of Montana and Wyoming, were not acclimatized to the heat and humidity of the Southern Plains, and within two months of their arrival, nearly two-thirds were ill.

On September 9, 1878, a large band under Dull Knife and Little Wolf broke camp and started home. After driving off a detachment of soldiers, they crossed into Kansas, where some warriors went on a rampage of murder, rape, and plunder. Above the North Platte River, they split into two groups, with Little Wolf leading his people to Montana where the ever-insubordinate Nelson Miles allowed them to settle quietly. Dull Knife, meanwhile, was forced to surrender his band near Fort Robinson, Nebraska, where they were interned pending transportation back to the Territory. Determined to die rather than return, they barricaded themselves in a barracks. With the tacit consent of Crook and Sheridan, the commanding officer, Captain Henry Wessells, cut off their food and water to force them into submission. The Cheyennes, however, had firearms concealed in pieces in their clothing, and on January 9, 1879, they began reassembling them. Late that night, they attacked the guards and fought their way out. Over the next few weeks, they were hunted down, and most were recaptured. Some were allowed to settle at Pine Ridge, just south of the Black

Dull Knife (seated) and Little Wolf were leaders of the Cheyenne Outbreak of 1878–79. They were two of the four "old men" or senior chiefs of the Northern Cheyennes. (Smithsonian Institute)

Hills. Others were returned to the Territory, although eventually they, too, were allowed to go to Pine Ridge or Montana (Monnett).

Another group pushed beyond endurance was the White River Utes of western Colorado. When silver was discovered in the San Juan Mountains in their territory, they were forced to surrender one-fourth of their reservation. This was followed by pressure from local citizens to seize the rest of their reservation and remove the Utes to the Native American Territory. Matters came to a head with the appointment of a totally incompetent agent, Nathan C. Meeker, who insisted they plow up their pony pastures and turn to agriculture. A confrontation between Meeker and a Ute medicine man called Johnson led to a scuffle and Meeker sent for troops. A detachment sent from Fort Fred Steele, Wyoming, the nearest post, was blocked at Milk river, and pinned down in a week-long siege before a relief column arrived. The Utes, meanwhile, had risen up, burned the agency, killed Meeker and nine employees, and carried off their families.

To avoid possible harm to the hostages, Interior Secretary Schurz enlisted the aid of Charles Adams, a former agent whom the Utes trusted, and Ouray, the powerful chief of the Uncompahgre Utes. Faced with Ouray's threat to unite all the other Ute tribes against them, the White River band surrendered and returned the hostages. The incident accelerated demands for removal of all Utes. Although some retained a small reservation in southwestern Colorado, the rest were removed to Utah (Utley and Washburn, 306–10).

The Cheyenne Outbreak and the Ute Rising signaled the end for the Plains Native Americans. Isolated incidents might occur here and there, but in reality the Native American Wars on the Great Plains were over, and the region rapidly developed. The Great American Desert, as it once had been called, was no more. In 1889 alone, Wyoming,

Montana, and Idaho were admitted as states, and Dakota Territory was divided into North and South to create two states. Utah followed in 1896, the delay caused primarily because the Mormon theocracy that governed the territory had to readjust to accommodate federal law and policy. Then, in 1906, the Native American Territory was consolidated with the Territory of Oklahoma, which was admitted as a state one year later.

The reality of the situation was summed up by Schurz, who wrote in the *National Review* that every part of the country was becoming accessible by railroad, and that gave the land conventional economic value. The Native Americans, he said, would have to face that reality. Meanwhile, because many whites still advocated extermination, the Native Americans needed government protection ("Present Aspects").

In 1887, Congress approved the General Allotment Act, better known as the Dawes Act, after its sponsor, Senator Henry Laurens Dawes of Massachusetts. The Act terminated tribal ownership of reservation lands, allocating 160 acres (.65 km^2) to every Native American head of household, 80 acres (0.3 km^2) to single persons over 18 years old and orphans under 18, and 40 acres (0.15 km^2) to all others under 18. Citizenship was offered to those who accepted the allocation and abandoned tribal life. The result of the act was two-fold: first, it attempted to destroy the base of tribalism by abolishing communal lands, and second, once the lands were allocated to all Native Americans on a reservation, many reservations would still have a vast amount of unallocated land that would be opened to settlement. This led to the loss of almost 100 million acres (0.5 million km^2) of Native American land, some 80 percent of what they held before the act went into effect (Utley, 1997, 121–22).

One of the reservations broken up under the act was the remnant of the Great Sioux Reservation created under the Fort Laramie Treaty. A commission composed of Govenor Charles Foster of Ohio, chairman, Senator William Warner of Missouri, and Crook, now major-general and commander of the

Military Division of the Missouri, met with the Lakotas in the spring and summer of 1889. Although Crook used diplomacy, he also led the Native Americans to understand that if they did not agree to hand over the land, the government would take it anyway. Adding insult to injury, once they signed away their land, the government reduced their appropriation. In desperation, many joined the Ghost Dance movement, which had originated in Nevada that year, and now was rapidly moving eastward across the plains (Robinson, 2001, 299–300).

An early Ghost Dance movement had originated among the Paiutes and was active in California and Oregon in the 1860s and 1870s before gradually fading away. It was revived in 1889 by a Paiute named Wovoka, who preached the dawn of a new era in which the Native American lands would be restored, and people would be reunited with their dead ancestors. Wovoka's message stressed peace, and the performance of a circular dance.

The very technology that the Native Americans had opposed for so long—telegraph and railroads—aided its spread, and soon it was embraced throughout the plains. Ancient tribal enemies set aside their animosities, and joined together in a religious euphoria, preparing for a world to come. It became particularly popular among the Lakotas, now reduced to total desperation. The government, sensing the threat of rising Native American nationalism, determined to stop it. At the Standing Rock Reservation, North Dakota, the movement centered on Sitting Bull. When tribal police went to arrest him on 15 December 1890, fighting broke out. Sitting Bull, several of his followers, and some of the Native American police were killed.

The Dakota Reservations were occupied by troops, and Oglala leaders at the Pine Ridge Reservation, in South Dakota, managed to contain the Ghost Dancers. At Cheyenne River, South Dakota, a large group of Ghost Dancers under Chief Big Foot panicked at the arrival of troops and fled westward toward the Badlands. They were rounded up and brought to Wounded Knee Creek on December 28. The army planned to march them to Pine Ridge the next morning, and put them on the train for Cheyenne River.

On the morning of December 29, the warriors were separated from the women and children, and searched for weapons. The soldiers were nervous, and many had been drinking the night before. A scuffle broke out over a rifle, a shot was fired, and the Native Americans began pulling out concealed weapons. The soldiers leveled their rifles and opened fire at point-blank range, killing about half the warriors in the first volley. Then four rapid-fire Hotchkiss cannons opened up with shrapnel. When it ended, the bodies of 146 men, women, and children were buried in a mass grave. However, many wounded later died, and relatives recovered the bodies of other dead, so the actual toll may have reached 300. The Native American way of life also died at Wounded Knee (Hoxie, 223, 694–97).

The Plains Wars now entered the realm of legend. Just as whites have mixed emotions over Custer, so too Native Americans have mixed emotions over their chiefs. Among the Kiowas, the animosity between the Satanta adherents and Kicking Bird adherents lingers to some extent even today. Quanah Parker, who after his surrender prospered as a rancher, businessman, and ultimately federal judge, remains a controversial figure among the Comanches. Red Cloud's grudging accommodation after the close of the Plains Wars causes some Oglalas to question his integrity. The defiant chiefs, however, have become symbols, particularly if they died resisting the government, or at least under questionable circumstances. Such were the cases of Crazy Horse, who was bayoneted to death at Camp Robinson in 1877, and Sitting Bull, both of whom had assumed almost mythical proportions even among the troops during the Great Sioux War.

After interviewing many Native American combatants for a final report to General Crook, Lieutenant Philo Clark noted (United States Department of War, record group 393, Sioux War, September 14, 1877):

Great prominence has been given Crazy Horse and Sitting Bull in this war; the good fighting strategy and subsequent muster by retreats being attributed to them, whereas they are really not entitled to more credit or censure than many others so far as plans and orders were concerned ....

There is no question that during this war, the two chiefs were, in fact, respected and charismatic leaders, Sitting Bull perhaps a little more than Crazy Horse. Dead, however, they have assumed cult status, as symbols of Native American resistance. The Lakotas, particularly the Oglalas of Pine Ridge, South Dakota, have cited the "Spirit of Crazy Horse," in asserting their identity, and their right to exercise their own way of life.

Today, the Native American continues to trouble the national conscience. Although all Native Americans born in the United States are citizens, in many cases they have been relegated to a secondary status, reduced to a permanent dependency on the federal government. Part of this is because a massive government bureaucracy exists on managing Native American affairs. "The fact is," General Crook once observed, "there is too much money in this Native American business ...." (Crook, November 28, 1871, Collection). That still holds true. Casino gambling has been extolled as the great cure for all Native American ills, but it is a mixed blessing. Some tribes have grown wealthy, but others have suffered. In 1999, an Oglala leader observed that the casinos at Pine Ridge bring large amounts of money to a tribal benevolent fund, but because so many members of the tribe gamble, the draw on that fund has increased proportionately.

No one seems sure how to address the situation of the Native Americans, and the Native Americans themselves are divided. Some insist that all reservations, government relief, and other programs separating them from the mainstream should be completely abolished, and the Native Americans should take their place as co-equal citizens, to succeed or fail on their own. Others contend

Mass grave at Wounded Knee. (Author's collection)

that they cannot exist without government help, and assistance is the least the government can do.

The question facing the United States is the same question facing any nation, where an alien people have displaced but have not assimilated or been assimilated by the indigenous people. It is a question that also faces Canada, Brazil, South Africa, Australia, and many other nations. The indigenous people are human beings with the power of conscious thought and action; they cannot be placed on a reserve and preserved unchanged forever as though they were a species of wildlife. Yet neither can the indigenous people withdraw from a modern, ever advancing world. How to assimilate them into the modern world, yet preserve their rights as human beings is the great question. So far, there have been no answers.

Principal Native American characters

Big Tree (c. 1852–1929), Kiowa subchief, convicted with Satanta of murder for his part in the Warren Wagon Train Massacre of 1871, was later paroled. Became a Baptist deacon, and a prominent leader of his community.

Black Kettle (c. 1810–68), Cheyenne peace chief, and leader of the band massacred by Colorado troops at Sand Creek in 1864. Killed by regular troops in the battle of the Washita in the Native American Territory.

Brave Bear (d. 1854), Lakota paramount chief, mortally wounded in the Grattan Massacre.

Crazy Horse (c. 1840–77), Oglala Lakota war leader, famed for his charisma, and for his pale complexion and red hair. Killed during a scuffle at Camp Robinson, Nebraska.

Dohasen (d. 1866), Kiowa paramount chief.

Dull Knife, also known as Morning Star (c. 1810–83), Northern Cheyenne senior chief, one of the leaders of the 1878–79 outbreak. Allowed to live near Pine Ridge, South Dakota, until his death.

Isa-tai (c. 1842–1914), Comanche prophet, one of the instigators of the Red River War of 1874–75.

Kicking Bird (c. 1835–75), Kiowa peace chief, kept the bulk of his people neutral during the Red River War. Died under mysterious circumstances, possibly of poisoning by the war faction.

Little Crow (c. 1803–63), leader in Minnesota Uprising of 1862. Killed by a citizen a year later.

Little Wolf (c. 1820–1904), Northern Cheyenne senior chief, led the Outbreak of 1878–79. Surrendered to Colonel Nelson Miles, and lived quietly in Montana until his death.

Lone Wolf (c. 1820–79), Kiowa war leader, succeeded Dohasen as paramount chief. Interned at Fort Marion, Florida, after the Red River War, died of malaria shortly after his release.

Medicine Bottle (d. 1865), leader in the Minnesota Uprising. Hanged at Fort Snelling, Minnesota.

Ouray (1820–80), autocratic paramount chief of the Uncompahgre Utes, ended the White River Ute uprising by threatening to unite all the other Utes against the White River band.

Parker, Quanah (c. 1845–1911), Comanche war chief, son of Peta Nacona and Cynthia Ann Parker. After the Red River War, he became a cattleman, businessman, and judge.

Red Cloud (1822–1909), Oglala war chief who fought the government to a standstill in 1866–68. He succeeded Spotted Tail as head chief of the Lakotas, and was prominent in tribal affairs until his death.

Satank (c. 1797–1871), Kiowa war leader. Arrested with Satanta and Big Tree after the Warren Wagon Train Massacre, he was killed by a guard at Fort Sill, Native American Territory.

Satanta (c. 1816–78), Kiowa war leader and diplomat, committed suicide in the Texas State Penitentiary, Huntsville.

Shakopee (d.1865), leader in the Minnesota Uprising. Hanged at Fort Snelling, Minnesota.

Sitting Bull (c. 1834–90). Hunkpapa political chief and leader of resistance in the early 1870s. Killed in a fight with tribal police.

Spotted Tail (c. 1823–81), Brulé leader, appointed by the government as head chief of the Lakotas in 1876. Assassinated during internal Lakota political dispute.

Standing Bear (c. 1829–1908), Ponca chief, initiated a landmark legal case that established Native American status as residents of the United States.

Washakie (c. 1804–1900), Shoshone paramount chief allied with the federal government during the Great Sioux War. Fort Washakie, Wyoming, was named in his honor.

Wooden Leg (1858–1940), Northern Cheyenne warrior, was prominent in the Great Sioux War. He later served as an army scout and a judge.

Glossary

cavalry Soldiers who fight on horseback.

colony A territory under political control of a state.

indictment A formal accusation that a person has committed a crime.

infantry Soldiers specifically trained to fight on foot.

massacre The typically atrocious act of killing a group of usually helpless people.

militia A military force composed of ordinary citizens.

negotiation A discussion intended to stop a dispute.

neophyte A beginner.

nomadic Roaming from place to place periodically in search of items necessary for survival.

piety Religious devotion or spirituality.

presidio A military post or settlement in an area under Spanish control.

rations A small food allowance for one day.

reservation An area of land managed by a Native American tribe under the United States Department of the Interior's Bureau of Indian Affairs.

scapegoat One who bears the blame for others.

shantytown A slum settlement of impoverished people.

For more information

American Indian Heritage Foundation
P.O. Box 750
Pigeon Forge, TN 37868
(703) 354-2270
Web site: http://www.indians.org
This foundation was established to provide
relief services to Native American people
nationwide.

Indian Wars Museum
P.O. Box 635
Bargersville, IN 46106
(317) 422-5147
Web site: http://www.museumsusa.org
This museum features a collection
of artifacts from the Native
American wars.

National Museum of the American Indian
The George Gustav Heye Center
1 Bowling Green
New York, NY 10004
(212) 514-3700
Web site: http://www.nmai.si.edu
This collection features artifacts and art
dedicated to the American Indian.

National Native American Law Enforcement
Association
P.O. Box 171
Washington, DC 20044
(202) 204-3065
Web site: http://www.nnalea.org

The association promotes cooperation
between American Indian law
enforcement officers, their agencies,
private industry, and the public.

Native American Heritage Association
12085 Quaal Road
Black Hawk, SD 57718
(540) 636-1020
Web site: http://www.naha-inc.org
This charitable organization is dedicated to
helping Native American families living in
need on reservations in South Dakota.

Rockwell Museum of Western Art
111 Cedar Street
Corning, NY 14830
(607) 974-5386
Web site: http://www.rockwellmuseum.org
The Rockwell Museum houses the largest and
finest collection of western art in the
eastern United States.

Web sites

Due to the changing nature of Internet links,
Rosen Publishing has developed an online
list of Web sites related to the subject of this
book. This site is updated regularly. Please
use this link to access the list:

http://www.rosenlinks.com/eaw/uspw

For further reading

Government documents and publications

United States

Barker, Eugene C., ed. *The Austin Papers*. Annual Report of the American Historical Association for the Year 1919. 2 vols. Washington: Government Printing Office, 1924.

Hancock, Winfield Scott. *Reports of Major General W.S. Hancock Upon Indian Affairs, With Accompanying Exhibits*. Washington: Government Printing Office, n.d. (1867).

Howard, James H. *The Ponca Tribe*. Smithsonian Institution Bureau of American Ethnology Bulletin 195. 1965. Reprint: Lincoln: University of Nebraska Press, 1995.

Lavender, David. *Fort Laramie and the Changing Frontier*. Washington: United States Department of the Interior, 1983.

Overfield, Loyd J., II, comp. *The Little Big Horn, 1876: The Official Communications, Documents and Reports with Rosters of the Officers and Troops of the Campaign*. 1971. Reprint: Lincoln: University of Nebraska Press, 1990.

United States Congress. *Report of the Joint Committee on the Conduct of the War, at the Second Session Thirty-eighth Congress. Massacre of Cheyenne Indians*. Washington: Government Printing Office, 1865.

United States Department of the Interior. Second Annual Report, Office of the Kiowa and Comanche Agency, Fort Sill, August 12, 1870. Manuscript copy in Myers.

United States Department of War. Office of the Adjutant General. Record Group 391 Series 757, Fourth Cavalry Expedition Records, Letters and Endorsements Sent and Orders Issued.

— Record Group 393. Special File. Military Division of the Missouri. National Archives Microfilm Publication 1495. Washington: National Archives, n.d. As follows:

Rolls 2–4. Sioux War, 1876–77.

— Office of the Surgeon General. Post Medical Report. Fort Griffin, Texas, 1867–1881.

— *The War of the Rebellion: A Compilation of the Official Records of the Union and Confederate Armies*. 130 vols. Washington: Government Printing Office, 1881–1898.

Wallace, Ernest, ed. *Ranald S. Mackenzie's Official Correspondence Relating to Texas, 1873–1879*. Museum Journal 10. Lubbock: West Texas Museum Association, 1968.

Individual states

DeLand, Charles E. *The Sioux Wars*. South Dakota Historical Collections 17. Pierre, S.D.: State Department of History, 1930.

Winfrey, Dorman H., and James M. Day, eds. *The Indian Papers of Texas and the Southwest, 1826–1916*. 5 vols. 1966. Reprint. Austin: Texas State Historical Association, 1995.

Spain

Jackson, Jack, ed. *Imaginary Kingdom: Texas as Seen by the Rivera and Rubí Military Expeditions, 1727 and 1767*. Austin: Texas State Historical Association, 1995.

Simpson, Lesley Byrd, ed., and Paul D. Nathan, trans. *The San Sabá Papers: A Documentary Account of the Founding and Destruction of San Sabá Mission*. 1959. Reprint. Dallas: Southern Methodist University Press, 2000.

Manuscripts

Bourke, John Gregory. Diary. 124 vols. United States Military Academy Library, West Point, NY.

Crook, George. Collection. Microfilm edition. Rutherford B. Hayes Library, Rutherford B. Hayes Presidential Center, Fremont, Ohio.

Hamby, Thorton K. "An Indian Raid in Young County, Texas, Oct. 13th, 1864." Elm Creek Raid Statements. Earl Vandale Collection. Center for American History, University of Texas, Austin.

King, Rufus, and Charles King. Collection. State Historical Society of Wisconsin. Madison.

Myers, James Will. Papers. Panhandle-Plains Historical Society. Canyon, Texas.

Schuyler, Walter Scribner. Papers. Henry E. Huntington Library and Art Gallery, San Marino, California.

Books

Primary sources

Babb, Theodore Adolphus. *In the Bosom of the Comanches: A Thrilling Tale of Untamed Indian Life, Massacre, and Captivity Truthfully Told by a Surviving Captive*. 1912. Reprint. Azle, Tex.: Bois d'Arc Press, 1990.

Bourke, John Gregory. *On the Border With Crook*. 1891. Reprint. Alexandria, Va.: Time-Life Books, 1980.

Boyd, Mrs.. Orsemus B. *Cavalry Life in Tent and Field*. 1894. Reprint. Lincoln: University of Nebraska Press, 1982.

Carleton, James Henry. *The Prairie Logbooks: Dragoon Campaigns to the Pawnee Villages in 1844, and to the Rocky Mountains in 1845*. 1943. Reprint. Lincoln: University of Nebraska Press, 1983.

Custer, Elizabeth Bacon. *"Boots and Saddles" or, Life in Dakota with General Custer*. New York: Harper Brothers, 1885.

Finerty, John F. *War-Path and Bivouac: The Big Horn and Yellowstone Expedition*. 1955. Reprint. Lincoln: University of Nebraska Press, 1966.

Fougera, Katherine Gibson, *With Custer's Cavalry*. 1942. Reprint. Lincoln: University of Nebraska Press, 1986.

Hunt, Frazier, and Robert Hunt. *I Fought With Custer: The Story of Sergeant Windolph, Last Survivor of the Little Big Horn*. New York: Charles Scribner's Sons, 1947.

Lee, Nelson. *Three Years Among the Comanches: The Narrative of Nelson Lee, the Texas Ranger*. 1859. Reprint. Norman: University of Oklahoma Press, 1991.

Marquis, Thomas B., (comp.) 1987. *Custer on the Little Big Horn*. Second rev. ed. Algonac, Mich.: Reference Publications, Inc., 1987.

— n.d. Int. *Wooden Leg: A Warrior Who Fought Custer*. Originally published as *A Warrior Who Fought Custer*. 1931. Reprint. Lincoln: University of Nebraska Press.

Miles, Nelson Appleton. *Personal Recollections and Observations of General Nelson A. Miles*. 1896. Reprint. 2 vols. Lincoln: University of Nebraska Press, 1992.

Mills, Anson. *My Story*, 2nd. ed. Washington: Press of Byron S. Adams, 1921.

Neihardt, John G., comp. *Black Elk Speaks, Being the Life Story of a Holy Man of the Oglala Sioux*. 1932. Reprint. Lincoln: University of Nebraska Press, 1965.

Parkman, Francis, Jr. *The California and Oregon Trail: Being Sketches of Prairie and Rocky Mountain Life*. 1849. Reprint. Alexandria, Va.: Time-Life Books, 1983.

Sherman, William Tecumseh. *Memoirs of General W.T. Sherman*. Rev. ed. 1886. Reprint. New York: Library of American, 1990.

Summerhayes, Martha. *Vanished Arizona: Recollections of the Army Life of a New England Woman*. 1908. Reprint. Tucson: Arizona Silhouettes, 1960.

Tatum, Lawrie. *Our Red Brothers and the Peace Policy of President Ulysses S. Grant*. 1899. Reprint. Lincoln: University of Nebraska Press, 1970.

Terry, Alfred Howe. *The Field Diary of General Alfred H. Terry: The Yellowstone Expedition – 1876*. 2nd ed. Bellevue, Nebr.: The Old Army Press, 1970.

Tibbles, Thomas Henry. *Buckskin and Blanket Days: Memoirs of a Friend of the Indians*. 1957. Reprint. Lincoln: University of Nebraska Press, 1973.

— *Standing Bear and the Ponca Chiefs*. 1880. Reprint. Lincoln: University of Nebraska Press, 1995.

White, David A., comp. *News of the Plains and Rockies, 1803–1865: Original narratives of overland travel and adventure selected from the Wagner-Camp bibliography of Western Americana.* 8 vols. and supplement. Spokane: The Arthur H. Clark Company, 1996–2001.

Secondary sources

Bolton, Herbert Eugene. *The Hasinais: Southern Caddoans as Seen by the Earliest Europeans.* Norman: University of Oklahoma Press, 1987.

"Brazos" (pseud.). *The Life of Robert Hall, Indian Fighter and Veteran of Three Great Wars. Also Sketch of Big Foot Wallace.* 1898. Reprint. Austin: State House Press, 1992.

Brice, Donaly E. *The Great Comanche Raid: Boldest Indian Attack of the Texas Republic.* Austin: Eakin Press, 1987.

Brown, Dee. *The Fetterman Massacre.* 1962. Reprint. Lincoln: University of Nebraska Press, 1971.

Carley, Kenneth. *The Sioux Uprising of 1862.* St. Paul: Minnesota Historical Society, 1976.

Fontana, Bernard L. *Entrada: The Legacy of Spain and Mexico in the United States.* Tucson: Southwestern Parks and Monuments Association, 1994.

Fox, Richard Allan, Jr. *Archaeology, History, and Custer's Last Battle: The Little Bighorn Reexamined.* Norman: University of Oklahoma Press, 1993.

Greene, Jerome A. *Yellowstone Command: Colonel Nelson A. Miles and the Great Sioux War 1876–1877.* Lincoln: University of Nebraska Press, 1991.

Grinnell, George Bird. 1956. *The Cheyenne Indians.* 2 vols. 1923. Reprint. Lincoln: University of Nebraska Press, 1972.

— *Fighting Cheyennes.* 1915. Reprint. Norman: University of Oklahoma Press.

Gray, John S. *Centennial Campaign: The Sioux War of 1876.* 1976. Reprint. Norman: University of Oklahoma Press, 1988.

Haley, James L. *The Buffalo War: The History of the Red River Indian Uprising of 1874.* 1976. Reprint. Norman: University of Oklahoma Press, 1985.

Hoig, Stan. *The Battle of the Washita.* Garden City: Doubleday & Company, Inc.

— *The Sand Creek Massacre.* Norman: University of Oklahoma Press. 1976, 1961.

Hoxie, Frederick E. *Encyclopedia of North American Indians.* Boston: Houghton Mifflin Company, 1996.

Hyde, George. *Red Cloud's Folk: A History of the Oglala Sioux Indians.* Norman: University of Oklahoma Press, 1937, Reprinted 1987.

— *Spotted Tail's Folk: A History of the Brulé Sioux.* New ed. Norman: University of Oklahoma Press, 1974. Reprinted.

Lazarus, Edward. *Black Hills/White Justice: The Sioux Nation Versus the United States, 1775 to the Present.* New York: HarperCollins Publishers, 1991.

Leckie, William H. *The Military Conquest of the Southern Plains.* Norman: University of Oklahoma Press, 1963.

Mardock, Robert Winston. *The Reformers and the American Indian.* Columbia, Mo.: University of Missouri Press, 1971.

McChristian, Douglas C. *The U.S. Army in the West, 1870–1880: Uniforms, Weapons, and Equipment.* Norman: University of Oklahoma Press, 1995.

McFeely, William S. *Grant, A Biography.* New York: W.W. Norton & Company, 1981.

Monnett, John H. *Tell Them We Are Going Home: The Odyssey of the Northern Cheyennes.* Norman: University of Oklahoma Press, 2001.

Nye, Wilbur Sturtevant. *Carbine and Lance: The Story of Old Fort Sill.* 3rd ed. Norman: University of Oklahoma Press, 1969.

Parkes, Henry Bamford. *A History of Mexico.* 3rd ed. Boston: Houghton Mifflin Company, 1960.

Priest, Loring Benson. *Uncle Sam's Stepchildren: The Reformation of United States Indian Policy, 1865–1887.* 1942. Reprint. New York: Octagon Books, 1992.

Robinson, Charles M., III. 1992. *The Frontier World of Fort Griffin: The Life and Death of a Western Town.* Spokane, Wash.: The Arthur H. Clark Co.

— *General Crook and the Western Frontier.* Norman: University of Oklahoma Press, 2001.

— *A Good Year to Die: The Story of the Great Sioux War.* New York: Random House, 1995.

— *The Indian Trial: The Complete Story of the Warren Wagon Train Raid and the Fall of the Kiowa Nation.* Spokane: The Arthur H. Clark Co., 1997

— *The Men Who Wear the Star: The Story of the Texas Rangers.* New York: Random House, 2000

— *Satanta: The Life and Death of a War Chief.* Austin: State House Press, 1998

Sklenar, Larry. *To Hell With Honor: Custer and the Little Bighorn.* Norman: University of Oklahoma Press, 2000.

Tanner, Ogden, and the Editors of Time-Life Books. *The Canadians.* Alexandria, Virginia: Time-Life Books, 1977.

Taylor, Colin F. *Native American Weapons.* Norman: University of Oklahoma Press, 2001.

Thrapp, Dan L. *Encyclopedia of Frontier Biography.* 3 vols. 1988. Reprint. Lincoln: University of Nebraska Press, 1991.

Utley, Robert M. 1988. *Cavalier in Buckskin: George Armstrong Custer and the Western Military Frontier.* Norman: University of Oklahoma Press.

— (ed.) *Encyclopedia of the American West.* New York: Wing Books, 1997.

— *Frontier Regulars: The United States Army and the Indian, 1866–1891.* 1973. Reprint. Lincoln: University of Nebraska Press, 1984.

— and Wilcomb E. Washburn. *The American Heritage History of the Indian Wars.* 1977. Reprint. New York: Bonanza Books, 1982.

Stallard, Patricia Y. *Glittering Misery: Dependents of the Indian Fighting Army.* Fort Collins, Colo.: Old Army Press, 1978.

Weddell, Robert. *The San Sabá Massacre: Spanish Pivot in Texas.* Austin: University of Texas Press, 1964. Reprinted 1988.

Articles

Primary sources

Anonymous. "Ashley-Ricaree Fight, 1823." 1823. Reprint. White, *News of the Plains and Rockies 1803–1865.* Vol. 1 (1996): 152–60.

Plummer, Rachel. "Narrative of Twenty-one Months Servitude As a Prisoner Among the Comanchee [sic] Indians." 1844. Reprint. White. *News of the Plains and Rockies 1803–1865.* Vol. 3 (1997): 321–35.

Schurz, Carl. "Present Aspects of the Indian Problem." *North American Review.* Vol. 133, no 296 (July 1881): 1–24.

Secondary sources

Barton, Henry W. "The Anglo-American Colonists Under Mexican Militia Laws." *Southwestern Historical Quarterly.* Vol. 65, no. 1 (July 1961): 61–71.

Hanson, Charles. "Thoughts on the Mountain Man and the Fur Trade." *Museum of the Fur Trade Quarterly.* Vol. 35, no. 4 (Winter 1999): 2–8.

Robinson, Charles M., III. 1993. "Blundering on the Plains: Hancock's War." *Old West.* Vol. 29, no. 4 (Summer): 28–34.

Newspapers

Army and Navy Journal

St. Louis *Missouri Democrat*

Index

About the authors

Professor Robert O'Neill is the series editor of Early American Wars. His wealth of knowledge and expertise shapes the series content and provides up-to-the-minute research and theory. Born in 1936 an Australian citizen, he served in the Australian army (1955–68) and has held a number of eminent positions in history circles, including the Chichele Professorship of the History of War at All Souls College, University of Oxford, 1987–2001, and the Chairmanship of the Board of the Imperial War Museum and the Council of the International Institute for Strategic Studies, London, England. He is the author of many books, including works on the German army and the Nazi party, and the Korean and Vietnam wars. Now based in Australia on his retirement from Oxford, he is the Chairman of the Council of the Australian Strategic Policy Institute.

Charles M. Robinson III, a native of Texas, is a history instructor at South Texas Community College and the author of twelve books, primarily on the American West. His most recent book, General Crook and the American Frontier, was released by the University of Oklahoma Press in October 2002. His book *Bad Hand: A Biography of General Ronald S. Mackenzie,* won the Texas State Historical Commission's prestigious T.R. Fehrenback Award, and was honored by a resolution from the Texas House of Representatives.